Binge Drinking

ISSUES

Volume 93

Editor

Craig Donnellan

Independence

Educational Publishers
Cambridge

First published by Independence
PO Box 295
Cambridge CB1 3XP
England

British Library Cataloguing in Publication Data
Binge Drinking – (Issues Series)
I. Donnellan, Craig II. Series
362.2'92'0941

ISBN 1 86168 301 4

Printed in Great Britain
MWL Print Group Ltd

Typeset by
Claire Boyd

Cover
The illustration on the front cover is by
Pumpkin House.

CONTENTS

Chapter One: Alcohol

The massive cost of Britain's binge drinking	1
Alcohol	3
What's what? and how much is too much?	4
Binge drinking Britons	5
How much is too much?	5
Drinking	6
Alcohol and the body	7
Alcohol and health	8
Binge drinking – are attitudes changing?	10
Alcohol and the law	11
Generation Alcopop	12
Alcohol and young people	13
A rural battle with the bottle	14
Nine children a day go to hospital for alcohol abuse	15
Young people and alcohol	16
Drinking to excess rising among women	18
'Ladettes' clog casualty units after catfights	19
Alcohol and crime	20
Call for pubs to cover cost of policing drunks	21
Drink, drugs and driving	22
Alcohol advertising	23
Alcohol and the night-time economy	24
24-hour drinking 'will fuel crime'	25
Drinking, crime and disorder	25
Alcohol sharpens your brain, say researchers	26
Responsible drinking	27

Chapter Two: Confronting Alcohol Abuse

Alcohol	28
Sensible drinking	29
Living with a drinker	30
Doctors see an alcoholic a day	31
The NACOA Helpline	32
Drinking problems 'are out of control'	33
Tips for cutting down	34
Alcohol harm reduction strategy: main points	35
Teenagers to help tackle under-age drinking	36
Double drink prices, urge doctors	37
Got a drink problem?	38
Wide-eyed and legless?	39
More young people get help for drink problems on-line	39
Key Facts	40
Additional Resources	41
Index	42
Acknowledgements	44

Introduction

Binge Drinking is the ninety-third volume in the **Issues** series. The aim of this series is to offer up-to-date information about important issues in our world.

Binge Drinking looks at the use of alcohol in society and ways of seeking help for alcohol problems.

The information comes from a wide variety of sources and includes:
Government reports and statistics
Newspaper reports and features
Magazine articles and surveys
Website material
Literature from lobby groups
and charitable organisations.

It is hoped that, as you read about the many aspects of the issues explored in this book, you will critically evaluate the information presented. It is important that you decide whether you are being presented with facts or opinions. Does the writer give a biased or an unbiased report? If an opinion is being expressed, do you agree with the writer?

Binge Drinking offers a useful starting-point for those who need convenient access to information about the many issues involved. However, it is only a starting-point. At the back of the book is a list of organisations which you may want to contact for further information.

*****

CHAPTER ONE: ALCOHOL

The massive cost of Britain's binge drinking

A modern culture of 'over-drinking' has led to three in five men and one in five women downing a dangerous amount of alcohol

In the cold light of day, the statistics are inescapable: we are a nation of booze hounds, consuming a staggering amount of beer, wine and spirits in a destructive relationship with alcohol that is costing Britain billions of pounds a year.

A four-year government review into the nation's alcohol culture – from youths lurching through our high streets to housewives slurping wine in front of the television at home – has found a system that encourages people to drink until they fall down, with three in five men and one in five women putting away more than the maximum safe limit.

The huge cost of our obsession with alcohol and the inability of millions of people to drink in moderation will be laid bare in the Government's Alcohol Strategy Review, which will show that under-16s are drinking twice as much as 10 years ago and that new-style 'drinking warehouses' and super-pubs are encouraging a growing culture of

By Kamal Ahmed, Political Editor

over-drinking. Groups of young men and women regularly drink many times the recommended daily limit – the equivalent of about a pint and a half of normal strength beer – in one evening.

> *'People aged 18 to 25 are going out and drinking four or five times the recommended daily limit – actually going out to get drunk'*

One young woman told Home Office researchers compiling the report that, if she did not go out and 'get plastered', she felt that the

evening had been wasted. 'We really do feel that for some groups there is an increasing problem with alcohol misuse,' Hazel Blears, the Home Office Minister, said 13 March 2004. 'People aged 18 to 25 are going out and drinking four or five times the recommended daily limit – actually going out to get drunk. At the other end is the chronic drinking, which affects mainly older people.'

The report will say that 40 per cent of all hospital accident and emergency costs are linked to alcohol and that, between midnight and 5am, 70 per cent of all A&E admissions are alcohol-related. Alcohol-related treatment costs the NHS £1.7bn a year.

It will also highlight the huge criminal and social disorder problems linked to alcohol, revealing that there are 1.2 million incidents of alcohol-related violence every year and 360,000 incidents of domestic violence, perpetrated mostly by drunk men.

The Home Office will propose city-centre marshals to police problem areas, including taxi ranks and late-night bus stops, where much of the violence flares. The use of Tokyo-style 'bus loaders' in Manchester has cut disorder.

Blears said it was time for the alcohol industry to clean itself up and stop indulging in 'irresponsible promotions' such as 'drink all you can for £10' and 'happy hours' that last most of the evening.

'It should not be, "Come in here, stand up, slam it down your throat, and then we'll throw you out on the street for the rest of the public, the taxpayer, to pick up the costs",' said Blears.

She added that the Government was willing to consider putting warning signs on bottles and messages about how many units each drink contained, as well as what was a safe limit. The report will also reveal that bingeing now accounts for 40 per cent of all drinking done by men.

New regulations for the advertising industry could bar it from creating a 'sexy' image around drinking. It is likely that the Government's media watchdog, Ofcom, will launch an inquiry into how alcohol is sold.

Blears said that pubs and clubs should be encouraging a more continental-style café culture which would bring higher-spending, older people back into city centres. They had often been frightened away at weekends because of drink-related violence.

In Manchester, the 20 police patrolling the city centre have been supplemented by 100 civilian public protection officers, who have helped to create a safer environment and reduce crime.

Blears, who backs the Manchester project and wants to see it extended, said that an increasingly lengthy 'adolescence' meant people were regularly drinking more. 'There is greater disposable income, people are settling down later, getting married later, having children later,' said Blears. 'People's adolescence, if you like, is lasting for longer.'

This, she said, had led to huge growth in the night-time economy. The value of the drinks industry to Britain is now more than £30bn, creating more than 1 million jobs and £7bn a year in taxes.

'There is a big job to do changing some of the social norms around how we view drinking,' said Blears. 'It will take us quite a while to get there, and I am under no illusion that we can create a Mediterranean drinking culture in the next six months.

The Government will admit that the public often fail to understand the number of units a man and a woman can safely drink in a week

---

'We have to explain that you can have a great time without getting drunk. You'll be healthier, happier, have a better relationship with your friends. It's not cool to be throwing up in the street.'

The Government will admit that the public often fail to understand the number of units a man and a woman can safely drink in a week. Guidelines suggest 21 units for a man – equivalent to about 10 pints of beer – and 14 units for a woman.

'There is confusion about what a unit is,' said Blears. 'When it started, a unit was a small glass of wine. Now you go into a pub and ask for a glass of wine and you get a bucket of the stuff, and that could be the equivalent of two to three units.

'We need to look afresh at labelling, how much we can look to get on the product, how much at the point of sale, how much information can we properly give people about how much they are drinking and what the effect is on them.

'Information is the key and we need to explore the options. If you want people to make choices they have to have the power to make those choices, and that means information. Labelling and warnings may well be appropriate; it is about what works.'

■ This article first appeared in the *Observer*, 14 March 2004.

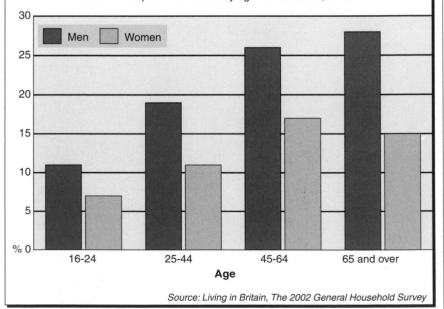

A summary of changes over time

When drinking questions were first asked on the General Household Survey in 1978, weekly-based measures of alcohol were reported. Questions relating to maximum daily amount have been asked since 1998, reflecting the move in 1995 from weekly-based to daily-based guidelines from the Department of Health. Longer-term trend data are therefore currently only available for weekly-based measures.

Percentage of men and women who had drunk alcohol on 5 days or more in the week prior to interview by age: Great Britain, 2002

Source: Living in Britain, The 2002 General Household Survey

Alcohol

Booze, drink, beverage, bev(y), swally

Alcoholic drinks consist mainly of flavoured water and ethyl alcohol (ethanol). They are made by the fermentation of fruits, vegetables or grains. Beer, lager and cider are usually about one part ethanol to 20 parts water although some brands may be twice as strong as others. Wine is about twice to four times as strong and distilled spirits such as whisky, rum and gin are about half water and half ethanol.

Below is some information on the relative strengths of various kinds of alcoholic drinks. The term ABV means 'alcohol by volume' or what percentage of the total liquid is actually alcohol.

The unit of alcohol measure is used to determine medical guidelines as to what are supposed to be safe levels of drinking for men and women per week. Safe drinking limits are given as daily maximums.

Authorities recommend that men should drink no more than three to four units a day and women no more than two to three units a day. It is also suggested that having one or two alcohol free days per week is wise.

What is a unit?

- One pint of normal strength lager (3-3.5%) is equivalent to 2 units
- One 275ml bottle of alcopop (5.5%) is 1.5 units
- A 175ml glass of 12% wine is 2 units
- A single measure of spirits (40%) is 1 unit[1]

These are measures of alcohol as might be bought in a restaurant or pub. Many drinks poured at home will be more generous and so contain more units of alcohol.

Alcopops

Most of these have an ABV of 4-5.5% with a range of units from 1.5-1.75 per bottle. The most well-known brands are the alcoholic lemonades and there are also alcoholic colas, fruit flavoured drinks and those using spirits such as vodka and tequila.

Spirits

Most standard 700 ml bottles of whisky, vodka or rum have an ABV of around 40% containing 25-30 units of alcohol.

Wine

Most wines are produced with an ABV of around 10-13% in a standard 750ml bottle containing 7-10 units of alcohol. Wines from hotter climates such as Italian and Californian wines tend to be stronger at 12 to 13% ABV while those from cooler climates such as Germany are usually 8 to 10%. Therefore a regular pub glass (125ml) of 12% wine is the equivalent of roughly 1.5 units. Fortified wines are even stronger, with drinks like Buckfast and Eldorado being as strong as 17%.

Sherry is usually produced with an ABV of 15-20% giving around 13-14 units of alcohol for a typical 750ml bottle

Cider

This varies in strength from the low alcohol varieties such as Strongbow LA with an ABV of just 0.9% up to the white ciders with an ABV of around 8.4%. Bottles usually contain 330ml; cans 440ml. A can of one of the stronger ciders contains around 2.5-3.5 units of alcohol.

Beer and lager

Most popular types of bitter beer are around 3.5 to 4.1% ABV – giving around 2-2.25 units for a pint and 1.5 to 1.75 units for a 440 ml can.

The strength of lager beers can vary widely and ranges from very low strength drinks like Barbican (0.02% ABV) to super strong' lagers at anything up to 10%. But like bitter beers, many popular lagers are around 3.5-4% ABV providing 1.5-1.75 units in a 440ml can and 2-2.25 units in a pint.

A different type of alcohol produced from wood (methyl alcohol) is used in methylated spirits and surgical spirit. Some down and out alcoholics ('meths' drinkers) drink this type of alcohol because it is cheap. Methyl alcohol is poisonous and can cause blindness, coma and death.

Unlike most drugs, alcohol has food value and supplies calories. One gram of alcohol supplies seven calories, almost twice the number of calories as one gram of carbohydrate. A pint of beer can supply as many calories as six slices of bread. Beer provides very little protein or vitamin and distilled spirits provide none at all.

Reference
1 Factsheet 8. *Health Impacts of Alcohol*. Alcohol Concern, Winter 2002/2003

- The above information is from Drugscope's website which can be found at www.drugscope.org.uk

What's what? and how much is too much?

Information from Lifeline

Alcohol is measured in 'units'. One unit is equal to a half a pint of ordinary strength beer, a pub measure of spirits or a pub measure of wine.

On the bottle, on the pump or on a list in a pub you will find the alcohol content of drinks. It is no accident that people with drink problems are fond of super strength lagers and ciders. Some of the super strength cans of lager are 9% alcohol. This means that one can of this 'loony juice' is nearly equal to three cans of ordinary lager. But they don't cost three times as much.

Experts now believe that men who drink no more than 3 to 4 units per day and women who drink no more than 2 to 3 units per day, are unlikely to harm their health. In fact, drinking between 1 and 2 units of alcohol a day can lower the risk of heart disease in middle-aged people.

2-3 units a day is a guide for a healthy adult. People at either ends of the age range and pregnant women should drink far less. But remember that there are times when even one or two drinks can be too much – e.g., if you are going to drive or operate machinery. It can also be dangerous to drink alcohol if you are taking certain types of medicine – check with your doctor or chemist.

2-3 units a day is a sensible guide, but of course we can't be sensible all of the time. If you go to the pub to celebrate a friend's birthday, you could easily end up drinking the number of units in one night that is recommended for a whole week. If this does happen, try and keep off alcohol for the next couple of days to allow your body to recover. Don't believe the myth about the 'hair of the dog'. Only time and not another drink will make you feel better.

Drinking more than 21 units a week (for a woman) and 35 units (for a man) puts you at greater risk of Liver Damage, Heart Disease, Brain Damage.

In terms of physical damage to the body and mind, excessive use of alcohol can be more dangerous than the limited use of pure heroin.

Now that's shocking isn't it?

Drink diary

Have a think about how many units you usually drink in a week. How many is it? Are you near the safe levels or are you way off? Keep a diary of a week's drinking. Record what you drank, on which days, at what times, where you drank it and who you were with. Add up the totals in units at the end of the week. This will give you an idea of your own drinking pattern.

■ The above information is an extract from *The Big Blue Book of Booze*, produced by Lifeline. For more information visit their website at www.lifeline.org.uk

© Lifeline

How much is a unit?

One unit	One unit	One unit	One unit	One unit
Half a pint of ordinary strength beer, lager or cider	1 small glass of wine	1 single measure of spirits	1 small glass of sherry	1 single measure of aperitifs

The table below gives strength and unit information for some of the more popular cans and bottles of drinks. As an approximate guide, 75cl bottles of table wine contain between 8 and 12 units and 70cl bottles of spirits contain approximately 30 units.

Drink	Size	Units
Bacardi Breezer	350ml bottle	1 3/4
Carlsberg Pilsner	440ml can	1 1/2
Carlsberg Special Brew	440ml can	4
Diamond White	275ml bottle	8.2
Fosters Export	375ml can	1 3/4
Harvey's Bristol (sherry)	750ml bottle	13 3/4
Heineken	440ml can	1 1/2
Hofmeister	440ml can	1 1/2
Holsten Export	440ml can	2 1/4
Holsten Pils	440ml can	2 2/3
Hooper's Hooch	330ml bottle	1 1/2
Jacob's Creek	750ml bottle	8 3/4
MD 20/20	187ml bottle	2 1/2
Skol	440ml can	1 1/2
Stella Artois	440ml can	1 1/2
Strongbow Super	440ml bottle	3 1/2
Tennants Extra	440ml can	2 1/4
Tennants Pilsner	440ml can	1 1/2
Tennants Super	440ml can	4
Thunderbird Red	750ml bottle	13
Two Dogs . . .	330ml bottle	1 1/3
Whitbread Best Bitter	440ml can	1 1/2

Binge drinking Britons

Binge drinking Britons don't know how much is too much. New poll reveals widespread public ignorance of safe drinking limits

British people are worried about the country's binge drinking – but few are aware of the safe drinking limits recommended by Government and medical experts, according to new research published as part of a campaign launched in December 2003.

The new MORI research reveals that 78% are concerned (43% 'very concerned') about binge drinking, drunkenness and disorderly behaviour among British people. Yet only 7% of men and 22% of women know that the current recommended allowances are 3-4 units and 2-3 units respectively.*

The seriousness of these figures is underlined by recent Government statistics revealing that almost 6 million people admit to binge drinking, with some 8 million drinking above the medically set limits.**

The unit system is further undermined by the lack of knowledge of how much booze is equivalent to a unit. The Office of National Statistics found in 2002 that only 50% of alcohol-consuming adults know that one unit is equivalent to half a pint of beer, with just over 60% knowing that a small glass of wine or single measure of spirits represents one unit.***

Furthermore, with stronger beers and wines and larger servings of many drinks than when the unit system was first introduced, it has become more difficult for members of the public to accurately monitor their consumption.

The new figures from MORI come just a few weeks after a Cabinet Office analysis of alcohol harm in Britain indicated that alcohol played a part in over 1 million fights, 19,000 sexual assaults and 360,000 domestic violence incidents each year – while costing the NHS £1.7 billion.

The new research is being published in a campaign launched by charities Alcohol Concern, Turning Point and the London Drug and Alcohol Network – as part of a series of projects urging the Government to publish and implement an effective alcohol harm-reduction strategy as a matter of urgency.

Commenting on the figures, Alcohol Concern's Chief Executive Eric Appleby says: 'While alcohol remains a Cinderella issue – a poor relation to drugs in terms of investment in treatment and education – it is hardly surprising that there are low levels of understanding about how much alcohol is healthy.

'We very much welcome the Government's commitment to a national alcohol strategy – but it was promised in 1998 and never came; it was promised for this summer and never came; then it was promised for this Autumn but we're still waiting. The sooner Ministers implement a national strategy in England, backed with significant investment, the sooner we can reverse the growth in binge drinking and reduce alcohol dependency.'

The Comic Relief funded campaign – called No Half Measures – will see other new research unveiled highlighting the impact of alcohol misuse on the country's emergency services, as well as recommendations for the National Alcohol Harm Reduction Strategy – including more easily accessible information about how to drink healthily. Advertisements calling for immediate action on alcohol misuse will also be displayed around the country.

Notes:
* MORI Social Research Institute. Results are based on interviews with 1,001 adults aged 16+, carried out by telephone between 19 and 21 September 2003. Data are weighted to the profile of the population of Great Britain.
** Interim Analytical Report, Cabinet Office (Strategy Unit), September 2003.
*** *Drinking: Adults' Behaviour and Knowledge in 2002*, Office of National Statistics, pages 28-30.

© *Alcohol Concern 2004*

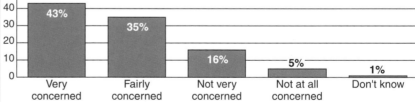

How much is too much?

How concerned are you personally about so-called 'binge drinking', drunkenness & disorderly behaviour among British people?

Category	Percentage
Very concerned	43%
Fairly concerned	35%
Not very concerned	16%
Not at all concerned	5%
Don't know	1%

Base: Adults aged 16+ (1,001)

As you may know, there is a recommended alcohol consumption allowance, measured in units. Do you know what the current recommended allowance is for you, per day or per week?

	Men	Women		Men	Women
0-1 unit per day	2%	3%	0-7 units per week	4%	4%
2-3 units per day	15%	22%	8-13 units per week	3%	4%
3-4 units per day	7%	3%	14 units per week	2%	10%
5-6 units per day	2%	1%	15-20 units per week	3%	2%
7-10 units per day	2%	1%	21 units per week	8%	2%
More than 10 units per day	-	*	22-30 units per week	6%	-
			31-50 units per week	1%	-
			More than 50 per week	-	*
			Don't know	44%	48%

Base: Adults aged 16+.
Men 439, Women 562

Source: MORI

Drinking

By Uttlesford Youth Forum, in Essex

Under-age

Sneaking in a drink while your parents aren't looking or downing several glasses to keep up with your friends may seem cool, but drinking alcohol under-age can damage your liver and get you into trouble.

In only two out of your seven teenage years is it legal to drink in pubs or clubs, buy alcohol from off-licences, or bring duty-free booze back from holidays. But many teenagers break the law and drink under-age. Some say it is because they are bored and have nothing better to do, some because it is their way of rebelling against authority, and others because they think it means they are mature and in control.

But is getting drunk out of your head or binge drinking really fun? The down sides of drinking too much are not pleasant and can be dangerous, such as losing your inhibitions, hangovers and dehydration (feeling grim and having headaches), throwing up or being embarrassed about your body being uncontrollable, and in the worst situation receiving medical care such as stomach pumping.

If you have never drunk alcohol, don't feel you're missing a lot.

Problems of excessive drinking affect everyone. It can cause abusive behaviour and lead to violence particularly where large groups meet. You can end up hurting people you care about or causing a serious accident.

Teenagers we spoke to for this article said they felt even more pressured to try a drink since the arrival of alcopops and spirit mixed drinks, and they didn't realise what they were or that they could be stronger than some wines and beers.

Peer pressure can be very strong, but it's not rude to say no to a drink.

Under-age people are still drinking in public places and being served in pubs and off-licences. ID cards are not always asked for, though they should be. Certain areas have ID cards issued through schools to

those over 16. At 17 you can apply for a provisional driving licence with a photo ID card that is accepted as proof of age.

If you ask someone older to buy you a drink from an off-licence, you can both get into trouble with the police, as buying a drink for someone who is under-age is breaking the law.

Remember, it is not rude to decline a drink. Having a drink will not make you seem more grown-up or improve your image, and binge drinking is not fun or clever, just expensive and will make you ill.

When can you drink?

16 or 17

You can buy or be bought beer or cider on licensed premises, but only for drinking with a meal in a restaurant area. It can't be drunk in a bar area.

Under 18

Except for 16- or 17-year-olds having a meal in a pub, it's against the law for anyone under 18 to buy alcohol in a pub, off-licence, supermarket or other outlet. It's also illegal for anyone to buy alcohol in a pub for someone under 18.

Peer presure can be very strong, but it's not rude to say no to a drink

---

18 or over

You can buy alcohol, but you might get asked for ID.

ID cards

You can use a provisional or full photocard driving licence to prove your age. You can also pick up application forms for proof of age cards in shops and off-licences.

What alcohol does & helplines

What does alcohol do?

Alcohol can help people feel relaxed and happy, but it is actually a depressant that slows down the way your body works.

It makes you clumsy and affects your reaction times. It can also make you do or say something you might regret, and it makes some people get violent.

Alcohol gets into your bloodstream and reaches your brain within minutes of having a drink. But it can take hours for the effects to wear off. What you've been drinking, how much you've drunk and your body size all influence the effect alcohol will have on you.

Drinking too much can make you pass out, and you could end up choking on your own vomit. Mixing different drinks, mixing drinks with drugs and drinking a lot in a short time can be very risky.

People who've drunk too much usually feel terrible the next day. A hangover makes you feel tired, sick and thirsty, and you'll have a headache. This is because drinking causes dehydration, and the kidneys lose too much water.

Health effects

While drinking can make you feel bad the morning after, it can also do long-term damage to your health. Too much alcohol can affect nearly every organ in your body – including your brain, skin and sex organs.

People who drink heavily are more likely to have an accident. Around half of pedestrians aged between 16 and 60 killed in road accidents would fail the breath test.

Heavy drinkers are likely to put on weight – which can cause heart disease, high blood pressure, diabetes and some cancers. Heavy drinking increases the risk of cancer of the mouth and throat, and the risk is made much higher if you also smoke.

Drinking too much can affect the way your body digests food and can give you stomach ache and increase the chances of getting ulcers.

Getting help

Around one in ten people in the UK have a problem with drinking. If you're worried about someone, there are people you can talk to. Ring Drinkline on 0800 917 8282 or ChildLine on 0800 1111

Alateen offers a helpline for young people with alcoholic parents or friends on 020 7403 0888

■ The above information is from youngGov, a part of the National Grid for Learning. For more information visit the web site younggov.ukonline.gov.uk

© Crown copyright 2002-2004

Alcohol and the body

Information from Alcohol Focus Scotland

Alcohol affects different parts of the body if you regularly drink to excess.

Skin

Alcohol dehydrates your body and your skin, often causing redness and blotchiness. It can cause the permanent enlargement of the blood vessels of the skin, producing a flushed colour.

Liver

When the liver has to deal with more alcohol than it can handle, it's likely that damage will occur. This can happen in stages.

Fatty liver: deposits of fat in the liver – full recovery is possible.

Alcohol hepatitis: inflammation of the liver – full recovery is possible.

Cirrhosis: a permanently scarred and damaged liver.

Stomach and oesophagus

Excessive use of alcohol tends to have a corrosive impact on the linings of these organs causing conditions such as:

Gastritis: an inflammation of the stomach cleared up by avoiding alcohol.

Ulcers: may not be caused by alcohol but are certainly irritated by excessive use of alcohol.

Reflux: can cause ulceration, tearing, bleeding around junction of stomach and oesophagus.

Pancreas

This is a large gland behind the stomach which secretes enzymes and releases insulin. Regular binge drinking can cause serious damage to the pancreas.

Acute pancreatitis: an inflammation of the pancreas. Causes severe pain with symptoms sometimes persisting even when alcohol is avoided.

Chronic pancreatitis: similar to the acute version and sufferers may also develop diabetes. This condition usually follows many years of excessive alcohol use.

Brain and nervous system

Persistent heavy drinking is often linked to a number of specific forms of brain damage.

Wernicke's encephalopathy: often confused with signs of intoxication – caused by a lack of thiamine (vitamin B1) and can be treated by injection of the vitamin, but is often undiagnosed.

Korsakoff's syndrome: can develop from untreated Wernicke's encephalopathy and is characterised by significant memory loss, similar to dementia. Improvement is variable, even with avoiding alcohol.

Heart and circulatory system

Heavy drinking can raise the blood pressure which increases the risk of heart disease and stroke.

Reproductive system

Heavy drinkers take longer to get aroused and longer to reach orgasm. Alcohol can affect a woman's chances of becoming pregnant. Men can become impotent.

■ The above information is from Alcohol Focus Scotland's website which can be found at www.alcohol-focus-scotland.org.uk

© Alcohol Focus Scotland

Alcohol and health

Information from the Institute of Alcohol Studies

In developed countries alcohol is one of the ten leading causes of disease and injury. Worldwide, alcohol causes 3.27 per cent of deaths (1.8 million) and 4 per cent of 'disability adjusted life years' lost (DALYS) (58.3 million). In developed countries, alcohol is responsible for 9.2 per cent of the disease burden.

Alcohol causes nearly 1 in 10 of all ill-health and premature deaths in Europe

The World Health Organisation's Global Burden of Disease Study finds that alcohol is the third most important risk factor, after smoking and raised blood pressure, for European ill-health and premature death. Alcohol is more important than high cholesterol levels and overweight, three times more important than diabetes and five times more important than asthma.

This level of alcohol-related death, disease and disability is much higher in men than women and is highest in Europe and the Americas, where it ranges from 8% to 18% for males and 2% to 4% for females.

Beside the direct effects of intoxication and addiction, world-wide alcohol is estimated to cause 20-30% of cancer of the oesophagus, liver cancer, cirrhosis of the liver, epilepsy, homicide and motor vehicle accidents.

The more a country drinks, the greater the harm from alcohol

The European Comparative Alcohol Study, financed by the European Commission, finds that as a country's alcohol consumption goes up and down, the harm done by alcohol goes up and down in parallel. This applies to all European countries. Further, the higher the alcohol consumption of a country, the greater the harm from alcohol. With the exception of Ireland, which has had an un-precedented and very recent rise in alcohol consumption, the top four European countries in alcohol consumption during the second half of the 1990s were Portugal, France, Germany and Austria. These, along with Italy, were among the top five countries with deaths from cirrhosis of the liver, a sensitive indicator of the harm done by alcohol.

The more an individual drinks, the greater the risk of harm

For all types of alcohol-related harm, including cancers, cardiovascular diseases and cirrhosis of the liver, the more an individual drinks, the greater the risk of harm. The annual risk of death from alcohol-related cancers (mouth, gullet, throat and liver) increases from 14 per 100,000 for non-drinking middle-aged men to 50 per 100,000 at 4 or more drinks (4 glasses of wine) a day. The risk of breast cancer by age 80 years increases from 88 per 1000 non-drinking women to 133 per 1000 at 6 drinks (a bottle of wine) a day.

Risk of drinking compared with non-drinking appears to begin increasing significantly at an intake of around 3 drinks per day for:

- Cancers of the oral cavity and pharynx; oesophagus; larynx; breast; liver; colon; and rectum
- Liver cirrhosis
- Essential hypertension
- Chronic pancreatitis
- Injuries and violence

Risks begin to rise with any drinking and increase further with increased intake.

Although a small amount of alcohol may reduce the risk of a heart attack, for many drinkers alcohol actually increases the risk of heart disease

One drink every second day gives almost all the protection that alcohol has on reducing the risk of a heart attack. Above two drinks a day the risk of death from heart disease goes up, with the more alcohol drunk, the greater the risk.

Whether consumed as wine, beer or spirits, it is alcohol that matters

A glass of wine, 250ml of ordinary strength beer and a single measure of spirits are all equal in their impact on health. The biochemical changes that might reduce the risk of heart disease result equally from beer, wine or spirits; they do not result from grape juice or wine from which the alcohol has been removed.

In the UK, deaths from alcohol are increasing. For example, there were over 4000 deaths from liver cirrhosis (the main cause of which in

Deaths linked to alcohol consumption

Deaths from selected causes linked to alcohol consumption

	1999	2001	2002
Men			
Mental and behavioural disorders due to alcohol	316	322	311
Alcoholic cardiomyopathy	111	103	90
Alcoholic liver disease	1,928	2,292	2,418
Chronic hepatitis, not elsewhere specified	16	23	17
Fibrosis and cirrhosis of liver	928	956	919
Accidental poisoning by and exposure to alcohol	91	94	60
Women			
Mental and behavioural disorders due to alcohol	149	145	124
Alcoholic cardiomyopathy	31	17	29
Alcoholic liver disease	1,026	1,172	1,199
Chronic hepatitis, not elsewhere specified	65	55	60
Fibrosis and cirrhosis of liver	772	736	763
Accidental poisoning by and exposure to alcohol	47	45	43

Source: Statistics on alcohol: England, 2004. ONS

the UK is alcohol) in 1999. Two-thirds of the deaths occurred in under 65s. Over the last 30 years, deaths from this cause have increased 7-fold in men, 8-fold in women. Cirrhosis now kills more men than Parkinson's Disease, more women than cancer of the cervix.

Health benefits of alcohol

There is evidence to suggest that light drinking may confer some health benefits on some people, though this is still a matter of dispute. The main health benefit claimed is reduced risk of coronary heart disease (CHD). However, this protection, if real, is restricted to middle-aged and older individuals in populations with a high risk of CHD, and even within these populations protection may be confined to certain subgroups. It is not certain that reduced risk of death from CHD results in longer life expectancy. At a population level, any protective effects of CHD are cancelled out by increases in other causes of death. There is no evidence to show that alcohol is necessary for health. Studies of lifetime abstainers show that they have a longer than average life expectancy.

In the UK, the Strategy Unit estimated that alcohol prevents around 20,000 deaths a year by reducing the risk of CHD, about the same as its estimate of the number of premature deaths caused by alcohol. However, the World Health Organisation estimates that globally alcohol is responsible for 1.8 million deaths per annum in net terms i.e with any lives saved by light drinking already being taken into account.

Other possible benefits of alcohol consumption have been identified in relation to ischaemic stroke, peripheral vascular disease, diabetes, gallstones and cognitive functioning and dementia. However, the picture remains unclear, and the evidence is stronger for some conditions than others. It is also suggested that alcohol may have some psychosocial benefits, such as lessening symptoms of stress. The evidence here is also inconclusive.

Impact of alcohol on the NHS

Alcohol is responsible for up to 150,000 hospital admissions each year in England and Wales.

Major alcohol-related health conditions contributing to hospital admissions

Chronic disorders
Gastrointestinal conditions
Cardiovascular conditions
Neuropsychiatric conditions
Cancers
Maternal and perinatal conditions
Annual hospital admissions (chronic): 34,000-91,000

Acute disorders
Acute toxic effects
Accidents and intentional assaults
Self-inflicted injuries
Annual hospital admissions (acute): 39,000-60,000

Note: hospital admission figures show the range of admissions of patients with a primary diagnosis or a primary and/or secondary diagnosis involving alcohol misuse. (Adapted from Strategy Unit Interim Analytical Report)

- Overall probably around 1 in 16 of all hospital admissions are for alcohol-related causes.
- Up to 35% of all accident and emergency attendances and ambulance costs are alcohol-related.
- Between 12 midnight and 5am, 70% of attendances are alcohol-related.
- At peak times in A&E Departments,
  – 40% of all attendees have a raised blood alcohol level
  – 14% are intoxicated
  – 43% are problematic drinkers.
- Common reasons for alcohol-related attendance at A&E Departments include:
  – violent assault
  – road traffic accidents

– psychiatric emergencies
– deliberate self-harm.

- In addition, 1 in 5 patients admitted to hospital for other reasons are drinking at hazardous levels.
- In 1993 Dr J. Chick reported that in urban hospitals in Britain 15-30% of male medical and surgical patients and 8-15% of women patients have alcohol problems.
- Between 1995 and 1997, Marshal et al conducted a prevalence study of current substance misuse amongst acute general medical admissions in a London hospital. 20 per cent of admissions were identified as substance misusers; the majority (72 per cent) of the identified patients having an alcohol problem. 19 per cent were currently using illegal drugs and 9 per cent were poly drug users.
- In 1997-98, the number of bed days in NHS hospitals in England where patients were admitted with a primary diagnosis of alcoholic liver disease was 106,943.
- A study at the Royal Bolton Hospital in 2000 found that in just one month, 600 bed days were occupied on the gastroenterology ward by patients with alcohol-related conditions. Average length of stay was 18.2 days.
- In the same hospital over a 6-month period, 21% of acute psychiatric admissions were alcohol-related, and in one year, 649 patients were referred to the alcohol liaison nurse.
- 1 in 5 patients presenting to primary health care are likely to be excessive drinkers, and based on the average list size, each GP will see 364 excessive drinkers in a 12-month period.
- Problem drinkers consult their GPs twice as often as the average patient.

■ The above information is an extract from the IAS factsheet – *Alcohol and health*. For more information and the full list of references, visit the Institute of Alcohol Studies' website: www.ias.org.uk

Binge drinking – are attitudes changing?

In the last six months, or so, there has been much reported in the press about the increase in alcohol intake and especially binge drinking

What is binge drinking?

Binge drinking is where people consume more than twice the recommended daily units of alcohol, in one session, at least once a week – which is the equivalent of at least a bottle of wine.

The recommended amounts are 3 to 4 units of alcohol for men and 2 to 3 for women.

Who goes out binge drinking more often?

It has been found, according to the Government's Alcohol Strategy Unit's interim report, published in September 2003, that:

'The prevalence of drinking in excess of the weekly recommended limits has increased in both sexes and in most age groups from 16 onwards. This increase has been most marked in those aged 16-24, particularly women.'

A study for an alcohol misuse charity, by the market analysts Datamonitor, has found that the average 18- to 24-year-old British woman consumes almost three and a half times as much alcohol as Italian women of the same age.

Another noticeable point from the report is how much more this age group drinks, compared with the female population as a whole.

'The average woman in the UK consumes 108 litres of alcoholic drink a year, 18- to 24-year-olds down 203 litres.'

In 1999 the amount young women drank, when they were out, was 172 litres a year: that shows an increase in 2003 of 18%. The study predicts that the trend will increase and that by 2007, young women will be drinking 242 litres! (19% increase.)

That is quite a chilling thought, isn't it?

Especially as it has always been the norm, previously in the UK, for men

to go to the pub and consume excessive amounts of alcohol but in 21st century Britain, that has changed! What is even more disturbing is the fact that young people do not recognise that the amount they drink regularly is 'binge drinking'. According to a report in the *Observer* recently a young 21-year-old student is shocked at the suggestion that she is a binge drinker and says:

'Having three glasses of wine in a night more than four or five times a month counts as binge drinking? That is not binge drinking. That's called having a social life. A little alcohol lightens you up. Obviously there are those who take it too far,

and they should be specifically targeted rather than heaping stigmas on normal girls who just want to have a laugh – like their male counterparts.'

In society today many young women are getting their careers settled before having a family Therefore they feel that as they work hard Monday to Friday, they can relax and celebrate the weekend. Their motto seems to be 'work hard, relax well'.

In towns and cities many new 'female friendly' bars are opening, where young women feel 'safe' about going in either alone or with their friends. Also, most of these bars have 'Happy Hour' with cheaper prices, or even '2 for the price of 1', that last for two or three hours. This encourages everyone, men and women, to drink more in a shorter period of time that in turn leads to binge drinking and drinking to excess that then can lead to anti-social and violent behaviour.

However, the market is particularly aimed at young women with the packaging of drinks in 'girly colours' and in bottles, which make them good for dancing. In many bars, customers have to ask for a glass because normally the bar staff just hands over the open bottle!

Another possible reason for the increase in drinking by young women is that nowadays there are many more different alcoholic drinks available – such as alcopop, cocktails, spirits and wines, instead of just beer, which is still mainly regarded as a man's drink.

The Strategy Unit is to publish its report soon, on new measures to reduce binge drinking and it is thought that proposals on strengthening the alcohol advertising code are expected to be included. This has come about following claims that a growing number of sexy, suggestive ads are being used to glamorise heavy drinking.

The current Advertising Standards Authority code forbids linking alcohol with 'sexual capabilities, popularity, attractiveness, masculinity, femininity or sporting achievements', or suggesting it is 'the main reason for the success of any personal relationship'. Brewers must also not encourage 'excessive drinking' or target under-18s. Last year the ASA upheld five complaints, including one for the alcopop Red Square, featuring a man's naked back adorned with scratch marks, which it decided 'referred to sex'.

The advertising agencies are very clever at disguising the product they are promoting in their television adverts. Often it is only at the end that the viewer is aware that the advert is for a particular brand of beer or spirity based drink. Tony Blair had already suggested that a levy could be placed on advertising to fund health campaigns because up to £600 million is spent on alcohol advertising and promotion annually in the UK, which is six times the budget for NHS alcohol treatment in England.

It is also though that the report will also clampdown on 'Happy Hour' by either restricting this to one hour during slow periods of trade – as they were originally intended.

Surely the best way would be to stop 'Happy Hour' completely?

It has also been reported in the *Times* online that:

'Brewers will also be told to label bottles with the number of alcohol units they contain. A campaign will be launched to demonstrate the benefits of continental-style drinking, where alcohol is served with food.'

At least five Whitehall departments are wrangling over what should appear in the final report. The Chief Medical Officer, Liam Donaldson, has made it clear, according to a report in the *Guardian*, that urgent action is needed. Alcohol causes more than 150,000 hospital admissions a year, while deaths from liver disease have risen eightfold in men aged 35-44 and sevenfold among women over the past 30 years.

'The average woman in the UK consumes 108 litres of alcoholic drink a year, 18- to 24-year-olds down 203 litres'

These are all excellent recommendations but surely the best way is through education. If children are given the facts at an early age, and this is reinforced at different times in their school years, they are then able to make informed choices when the situations arise. Then, in time, the statistics about alcohol-related illness and crime will improve and fewer young women and men will binge drink.

■ BNTL Freeway have produced 'Thinking about Drinking' for Key Stages 2 and 3, which are resources for teachers, giving the facts about alcohol. The resources are based on the National Curriculum with lesson plans and ideas. A new resource for Key Stage 1 is now available called 'Drugs and their Dangers' it introduces the concept of the dangers of drugs and alcohol to young children in a non-threatening way. It is a teaching resource based around three lesson plans, including kinetic learning activities and story.

■ The above information is from the magazine of BNTL Freeway. For more information see page 41 for their address details.

© BNTL Freeway

Alcohol and the law

Information from www.youthinformation.com

In the United Kingdom, there are strict laws on the sale of alcohol, on when people can enter a pub or bar where it is sold and on buying alcohol.

Generally it is illegal for a landlord or bar manager knowingly to sell alcohol to anyone under the age of 18. It is illegal for someone over 18 to buy or attempt to buy alcohol for someone under 18. It is also an offence for someone under 18 to buy or attempt to buy alcohol for themselves.

Anyone wishing to sell alcohol has to apply for a licence from a local licensing committee. Licenses can be issued for pubs, clubs, restaurants, temporary beer tents, off-licences etc., to sell alcohol at different hours of the day and to sell different types of alcoholic drink (e.g. just wine, or just beer). Because of the range of different licences which can be issued, there are also different ways in which the law can be broken. For example it would be illegal for a club licensed to sell beer and cider to sell whisky.

Below is a summary of the main age restrictions relating to drinking in licensed places:

■ Under the age of 14 children are not permitted into the bar area of a pub unless the pub has a children's certificate. In this case they can enter if they are accompanied by an adult.

■ At 14 you can enter a bar or pub but only if the landlord agrees and if you drink soft drinks (this can include low-alcohol beer).

■ At 16 you can buy beer, cider or perry (made from pears) in a restaurant or eating area of a pub where there is no bar, if you are ordering a main meal.

■ At 18 you can legally buy drinks in a pub, bar or off-licence. If you are having problems getting served in pubs and you are over 18 you could apply for a proof-of-age card from the Portman Group, an organisation set up by the drinks industry.

■ The above information is from the Information Toolkit for young people by the National Youth Agency. For further details, visit their web site: www.youthinformation.com

© The National Youth Agency

Generation alcopop

Heavy drinking among young people is not simply the booziness of adults brought forward, but a different phenomenon, suggests Godfrey Holmes

Teenage drinking has been seen as a 'rite of passage' on the journey from adolescence to adulthood. We feel more comfortable defining their problematic consumption as the same as heavy drinking by adults, but just acquired a bit earlier. That way, everybody – consumer, advertising agency, manufacturer – stays happy. The Government, feigning outrage, heartily endorses the £30bn-a-year industry that employs more than a million people.

But the problem of excessive drinking among young people differs in nature from that of other generations, and therefore needs to be tackled in a different way. The reasons why young people drink are different, as are the places they choose to drink in and the way in which they drink.

Tom Wylie, chief executive of the National Youth Agency and a critic of public policy surrounding 'the 24/7 leisure culture', places great emphasis on identity formation as a factor in young people's alcohol misuse.

He believes that young people do not resist the temptation of alcohol because it is the custom and will of the majority.

Sign of maturity

Teenagers feel they must demonstrate they are able to drink because it 'looks cool'. Alcohol is used as a signifier: many intoxicated young women are proud of the fact that they are behaving very differently from the way their mums and grandmothers did in their youth.

Wylie says young people use alcohol as a means to manage their anxieties, as 'a type of self-medication'. Teenagers have to worry about so many things, including peer pressure, sexuality, periods, acne, bullying, drugs, homework, exams, boredom, a lack of money and impending unemployment.

As two Year 10 students recently told a television reporter: 'Drink makes me feel good about myself. Things are better when I am drunk.'

Another key difference between young drinking and drinking over the age of 25 is visibility. A hundred years ago, working men used to drink heavily in smoke-filled saloons after collecting their wages.

The problem of excessive drinking among young people differs in nature from that of other generations, and therefore needs to be tackled in a different way

---

But that atmosphere does not suit today's young revellers. They want to be seen. They swarm in packs from pub to club and back, taking advantage of happy hours and the all-you-can-drink promotions on offer.

Alun Michael, minister for rural affairs and a former youth worker, believes adolescent drinking stands out in the countryside because of the lack of competing attractions. 'There is a high tolerance of drinking among (rural) parents, which is affecting attitudes,' he says.

Unique drinking habits

Young people's drinking habits also separate them from the over-25s.

Their preference for vodkas, cocktails and alcopops; drinking straight from the bottle (partly to rule out spiking and date rape); drinking to the accompaniment of mobile phones; and going out to get deliberately drunk is unique to the younger generation.

There is the important question of availability of alcohol. Young people have access to a wide choice of free alcoholic beverages at events such as parties and family celebrations.

Parents rarely notice, or criticise, their son or daughter for having a secret stash.

It would be fanciful to imagine today's young binge drinkers changing their ways when they are 25. Their bodies and minds might already be too dependent on alcohol.

As early as 1987, the Home Office Working Group on Young People and Alcohol provided most of the analysis of the problem, and many of the answers, but these were not implemented. Although that opportunity was missed, there is still time to influence, and perhaps to restrain, tomorrow's eager customers for 'a drink'.

■ Godfrey Holmes is the author of *Alcohol Among Young People: Obtaining the Full Measure*. For 25 years he has worked with young people at risk, many of them in care.

■ The above information is from *Young People Now* magazine. For more information visit their website: www.ypnmagazine.com

Alcohol and young people

Information from Alcohol Focus Scotland

Most of us start to experiment with alcohol when we're in our teens with few problems. However, alcohol can cause major problems for some young people. A great deal of these problems arise as a result of drinking excessively on single occasions.

What is alcohol?

Alcohol is a depressant drug, meaning that it slows down the brain and subsequently the other functions of the body. We measure our alcohol consumption in units, so the more units we drink the more our brain slows down. This may lead to changes in how we think, feel and behave.

What sort of changes?

Here are some examples:
2 Units = Increased confidence, relaxed, slowed reaction times.
4 Units = Increased confidence, impaired judgement.
More Units = Dizziness ▸ slurred speech ▸ loss of self control ▸ staggering ▸ loss of memory ▸ sleepiness ▸ coma ▸ death.

What are the risks and consequences?

Alcohol has a stronger effect on young people because of their age, smaller bodies and lack of experience with alcohol. In young people, smaller amounts of alcohol will therefore lead to higher risks. These can include:

- Aggression, arguments and fights – this could lead to a criminal record.
- Unplanned and/or unprotected sex – possibility of sexually transmitted infections and pregnancy.
- Other drugs – increased risk of trying other substances when drunk.
- Accidents – many young people drink outside therefore they can easily be knocked down or fall asleep and suffer from hypothermia.

Drinking among pupils

The proportion of pupils who had drunk in the last week increased with age (5% of 11-year-olds compared with 47% of 15-year-olds).

Percentage of pupils who drank alcohol last week, by sex and age

Source: Smoking, drinking and drug use among young people in England in 2002, National Centre for Social Research and the National Foundation for Educational Research, Crown copyright

- Overdose – it's possible, particularly for young people, to overdose on alcohol. Large amounts of alcohol can lead to drowsiness and/or coma with a high risk of choking on their own vomit.
- Alcohol poisoning – large quantities of alcohol taken in a short space of time can lead to alcohol poisoning. More than 1,000 young people are admitted to hospitals every year with alcohol poisoning.

Alcohol and the body

Females have less water in their bodies than males. So, when females drink alcohol they have less water to dilute the alcohol, which means it's more concentrated in the female body. This is one of the reasons why females get drunk quicker than males, on the same amount of alcohol.

Alcoholic drinks are high in calories but have no nutritional value.

There is no cure or way of sobering up – black coffee, cold shower, etc., are all myths. Time is the only thing which will make you sober. To become sober, your body needs to reduce the amount of alcohol in your bloodstream, your liver is the organ responsible for doing this but can only do this at roughly the speed of one unit per hour. There is no known way of speeding this up.

A hangover is basically alcohol dehydrating the body. The only sure way to avoid a hangover is not to drink too much.

Anything else I should know?

Remember – alcohol is widely used in our society and this can sometimes result in us forgetting that it's a drug. Individuals are expected to take responsibility for their drinking and for their behaviour afterwards.

If you're concerned about your own or someone else's drinking, contact Alcohol Focus Scotland for further information or information on the alcohol advice agency nearest to you.

Essential safety information

- Never leave someone unattended who is drunk, especially if they're starting to fall asleep. If you're unable to rouse the person, you should:
- Get an adult – if no adults are available, dial 999. Don't worry about being 'caught' drinking – people will be more interested in the life which is at risk!
- Turn the person onto their side (recovery position) so that if they vomit, they won't choke.

■ The above information is from Alcohol Focus Scotland's website: www.alcohol-focus-scotland.org.uk
© Alcohol Focus Scotland

A rural battle with the bottle

Young drinkers are becoming a feature of country life. Bryony Gordon reports

Hannah is 14 years old and she drinks half a litre of vodka every Friday night. Older friends buy it for her, and she mixes it with cola or cherryade. She spends her school lunch money – £20 a week – on alcohol. 'I used to drink during the week, too, but my parents realised and I had to stop,' she says. 'Now, they make me go to counselling once a week, but I still go to the park to drink at weekends.'

Hannah lives in Halstead, a small town in Essex. She is one of an increasing number of teenagers in rural and suburban areas who are out-drinking those who live in inner cities. A study by the Schools Health Education Unit at Exeter University revealed in April 2004 that 44 per cent of 14- to 15-year-olds living in villages drink between one and 13 units of alcohol a week, compared with 40 per cent of those living in towns.

While many people will be surprised by the unit's findings, experts in alcohol abuse are not. 'Living in a rural area does not necessarily protect against alcohol abuse,' says Andrew McNeill, the director of the Institute of Alcohol Studies. 'Drink is just as freely available and, since there are fewer alternative activities for teenagers who live in the country, the motivation to get alcohol may be higher.' Leo Lixenberg of Alcohol Concern agrees. 'I think another factor is that, in villages, it is easier to buy drink from small off-licences. Parents may also believe that it is safer to let their children out unsupervised in quieter areas.'

Cordelia describes her home as 'in the middle of nowhere in South Wales'. She is 18, but has been drinking with friends locally since she was 13. 'There is nothing to do here but get drunk in the local pub – the nearest leisure complex is a half-hour drive,' she says. 'When I was 14, it was easy to walk into the local pub and ask for a pint because they knew who I was. I remember trying to do the same at a bar in Oxford and being refused. It didn't make sense.

'My parents have always been very trusting of me. They've been happy for me to walk home at night because they know there is nobody around and anyone who is, we're probably friends with. But if I go to London for a weekend, I have to call them every hour on the hour, so they know I am safe.'

Matt, who is 16 and lives in a village just outside Cambridge, says he can easily knock back nine or 10 pints during an evening out.

'It always surprises me when I speak to my friends who live in London, because there doesn't seem to be so much of a drinking culture there, despite all the bars. Instead,

---

'Drink is just as freely available and, since there are fewer alternative activities for teenagers who live in the country, the motivation to get alcohol may be higher'

---

they tend to go to the cinema or round to friends' houses. But if I want to do that, I have to get my parents to drive me for 40 minutes. The easiest thing is for all of us to meet in the pub.'

Drugs, too, seem to be an issue among teenagers who live in rural areas. Hannah says that many of her friends take ecstasy. 'It's naive of adults to think that moving out of a city will protect their children from drugs and alcohol,' she says.

'They have to remember that in places like Halstead, there is absolutely nothing to do. We've got no attractions. There is a youth centre, but it's only open on Thursdays and the cinema has just shut down. So more or less everyone over the age of 12 drinks. It's the norm.'

However, it is not the norm for Melita, who lives in central London and is the same age as Hannah.

'I don't drink and neither do my friends,' she says. 'Instead, we go to the movies, roller-skating in the park or shopping. I'd rather go to Starbucks for a coffee than to a pub.'

Even if she wanted to go out drinking, her parents wouldn't permit it. 'They won't even let me get my ears pierced, let alone go out in London by myself. They think that it's far too dangerous.'

© *Telegraph Group Limited, London 2004*

Nine children a day go to hospital for alcohol abuse

Nine children a day are admitted to hospital in England for binge drinking, it is revealed today 27 April 2004.

Department of Health figures show that 3,322 children aged between 11 and 15 were admitted for alcohol-related problems. Some 2,760 were taken in for mental and behavioural disorders, with 562 suffering from alcohol's toxic effects.

Paul Burstow, the Liberal Democrat health spokesman who was given the statistics in a Parliamentary written answer, said: 'Teenage binge drinking is out of control. Alcohol abuse amongst teenagers is storing up huge long-term health costs. The number of children turning up in hospital is shocking.'

He accused ministers of 'dithering' and said the Government's recent alcohol strategy was 'failing to get to grips with the binge culture which is putting the lives and health of many teenagers at risk'. This month a 17-year-old public schoolboy choked to death on his own vomit after drinking beer, vodka and tequila on a school trip to Hamburg. Nicholas Ireland, from Weybridge, Surrey, was with 12 other pupils from King's College School, Wimbledon. Tony Blair's son Euan and Prince Harry have also been involved in binge drinking.

However, it is binge drinking among girls that is causing most concern. The 2003 Salvation Army Alcohol Awareness Survey showed that 22 per cent of girls aged 14 to 17 binge drink – compared to 19 per cent of boys – with drunkenness often leading to unprotected sex.

Among teenage girls, 60 per cent said their first alcoholic drink was premixed, like alcopops. Only 40 per cent knew that premixed drinks had a higher alcohol content than beer.

John Dalziel, a Salvation Army spokesman, said: 'Because of the marketing of the premixed drinks to

By Sarah Womack, Social Affairs Correspondent

teenagers, they're very attractive. They're well packaged, they're pretty, they're fashionable and they're mixing all their favourite childhood drinks like milk, lemonade and Coca-Cola with spirits.' The number of teenagers binge drinking has doubled in less than 10 years and more than half of all 15- to 16-year-olds have drunk more than five units in one session in the past month.

At Alder Hey Hospital in Liverpool, alcohol poisoning in the under-16s rose from 20 cases in 1985 to almost 200 in 1995, a pattern repeated across Britain.

Kim Williams, the lead nurse in the casualty department, said staff treated about four cases a week among children under 15, most of them girls.

She said: 'Girls dress up and look older so they can get hold of alcohol and get served in off-licences. There is no one teaching them about alcohol in school, like school nurses.

'In the last 18 months we have seen a 10 per cent increase in children admitted. We will have one young person who got really drunk and got to hospital but they were often in a gang of five or six, and we do not see the others.

'Often the young person is found drunk in a car park, field, or street. Their friends have got frightened and left them alone. We are about to start a brief intervention clinic where we invite them back to ask them why they ended up in hospital. We try not to make it a lecture, so we ask them how they felt the next day, how they looked and talk about the danger aspects. Many have turned up with injuries.'

She said the most worrying aspect was that teenagers were drinking to get drunk.

Alcohol abuse is costing £20 billion a year and almost six million people, mainly under 25, binge drink every week, according to the Government's alcohol harm reduction strategy. Yet ministers are pressing ahead with relaxing licensing laws next year, fuelling fears that anti-social behaviour will increase.

Ian Gilmore, the chairman of the Royal College of Physicians' alcohol committee, said the voluntary nature of the strategy, in which brewers, pubs and supermarkets take part in a range of initiatives with Government bodies and councils, would not have much effect.

© Telegraph Group Limited, London 2004

Hospital admissions

Number of young people aged 11-15 years admitted to NHS hospitals in England with a selection of alcohol-related primary diagnoses	Finished admission episodes					
Primary diagnosis	1997-98	1998-99	1999-2000	2000-01	2001-02	2002-03
Mental and behavioural disorders due to alcohol	2,457	2,326	2,950	2,918	2,921	2,760
Alcohol liver disease	-	-	1	1	-	-
Toxic effect of alcohol	895	737	764	739	674	562
Total	3,352	3,063	3,715	3,658	3,595	3,322

A finished admission episode is the first period of in-patient care under consultant within one healthcare provider. Please note that admissions do not represent the number of in-patients, as a person may have more than one admission within the year.

Source: Hospital Episode Statistics (HES), Department of Health

Young people and alcohol

Alcohol consultation with young people in England, 2004

Introduction

Turning Point carried out a consultation on alcohol with young people on behalf of Comic Relief from March 2003 to March 2004. We interviewed 98 young people from a range of different backgrounds, including ethnic minority communities, lesbian and gay groups, young offenders and asylum seekers. The range of settings were chosen to represent the range of circumstances in which young people find themselves, giving particular attention to vulnerable young people.

The aim of the study was to ensure that issues around young people and alcohol are kept on the political agenda in light of the publication of the national alcohol strategy for England. We hope that the views of young people presented within it will help inform the implementation of that strategy.

Turning Point consulted ten groups, totalling 98 young people between the ages of ten and 25. The average age was 15. Eighty-three of the 98 also completed a written questionnaire on alcohol. The consultation was led by Turning Point's Hungerford Project.

The young people that took part in this study had widely divergent views on alcohol, showed a high level of knowledge on the issues of alcohol and were very keen to suggest recommendations for policy and service delivery.

Young people's experience of alcohol

- 85% of young people had tried alcohol under the legal age of 18. A higher percentage of young women had never tried alcohol (16%) compared with young men (4%).
- Although the overwhelming majority of young people had used alcohol, the frequency with which they drank was substantially lower. Only 1% reported drinking every day and

16% reported not drinking at all. Nearly a quarter (22%) drank alcohol once a week.

- Beer (34%) and alcopops (28%) were the preferred drinks for young people, both as first drinks and in terms of continued use.
- 35% of young people had used alcohol in combination with cannabis on at least one occasion. Cannabis was mentioned across all age groups, with nearly a third (32%) of young people under the age of 16 having tried it.
- Young people said they drink mainly in the home or in friends' homes but not necessarily with the consent of their parents. For some young people, particularly for 14- to 16-year-olds, who consumed alcohol more regularly, their drinking took place outside the family home, in the streets, in parks or near where they lived.

Young people's attitudes towards alcohol

- Young people had a good understanding of the risks of alcohol, including harm to health, links with crime and engaging in general risky behaviour. This was not seen as a major disincentive to drink.
- Many young people identified a number of individual and social benefits associated with alcohol. Reasons given why young people drink are to have fun, to feel happy or relax. This was the major incentive to drink and rationale for subsequent behaviour. Some young people drink as a way of forgetting or solving problems.
- Young people strongly felt that their own drinking patterns were a matter of personal choice and not affected by peer pressure.
- Most young people felt that education about alcohol should start as soon as possible within a secondary school setting. One-quarter (23%) recommended that education should start for young people before they reached ten.
- Nearly six out of ten young people (58%) did not know where to go for help if they had a problem with alcohol.

Influence of others

- Peer pressure, breaking barriers and solving problems were all identified as contributing factors to problem drinking for other young people, if not themselves.

MUM, DAD - WE DO HAVE SOMETHING IN COMMON...

- Young people had very strong views on adult drinking behaviour and felt that they should set a good example and act as role models for young people.
- Young people felt that adult drinking was a bigger problem than drinking by young people.
- Young people saw parents/carers and teachers as the main source of information about the risks of alcohol. However, only a small minority said that they would be willing to talk to their parent/carer or a teacher about alcohol if they developed a problem themselves (14% and 10% respectively). Some young people felt that there was a conflict between teaching and providing support in other aspects of their lives. Others felt that parental or teacher disapproval would only encourage young people to drink more.
- Young people were more likely to approach wider members of the family, such as older brothers and sisters or uncles and aunts, for information on the risks of alcohol and for support if they developed a problem with alcohol.

Young people's solutions for addressing alcohol problems in England

- Young people felt that there should be more places to go for help if a person developed a problem with alcohol and that people had insufficient information on how to access treatment services.
- Young people wanted more information on the risks of alcohol and how to keep safe.
- They also felt that it was important to promote healthier alternatives to drinking such as improved access to leisure facilities and community activities.
- Over three-quarters favoured restrictions on advertising or a ban on advertising.
- Unpopular suggestions included ID cards (as it was thought that they would be difficult to enforce) and teachers talking to young people about alcohol problems.

Conclusions

Young people started drinking at a very young age and only a very small minority had never tried alcohol. Beer and alcopops seemed to be the most popular drinks both as a very first drink and in terms of continued use. Continued use was generally low, especially considering how early young people have their first experience of alcohol.

Young people had, in general, very mixed views on alcohol. Most of them were at least partly aware of the damage that alcohol causes to physical, mental and social health. Young people, however, also saw the social advantages of drinking alcohol, particularly in removing barriers. They enjoyed how it made them feel and liked the taste. There was also an expectation that certain events would involve the use of alcohol.

Most young people felt that education about alcohol should start as soon as possible within a secondary school setting

---

Young people felt that they had a good understanding of the harms associated with alcohol, particularly when alcohol could become a problem for a young person or adult, as well as their families. They had a good understanding of the difference between recreational and problematic use and the physical and social harms associated with alcohol misuse.

However, perhaps worryingly, young people did not apply that knowledge in relation to changes in their own drinking behaviour or to keep safe. Many young people took the active decision to drink and this was seen to be the norm and in line with society's general attitudes. In common with adults, there was a low understanding of the 'sensible drinking' message.

The role of parents was seen to be the most important factor, directly and indirectly, in influencing young people. However, there were mixed views on adult drinking behaviour and how this influenced them as young people. It was felt that the family could play a central role in talking to young people about alcohol, in reinforcing what young people learn at school and supporting young people who develop problems in drinking and helping to get over them. It was felt that young people would conceal their problems in relation to drinking behaviour, presuming that their parents would disapprove. There were concerns about misuse among parents and young people generally did not feel that parents who misused alcohol had the right to tell them not to drink. Young people felt more confident in approaching wider members of the family, such as older brothers and sisters or uncles and aunts.

Young people felt that education on the harm caused by alcohol should start early and be sustained during the young person's education. However, young people were often unwilling to approach teachers for advice and guidance on alcohol. Many did not trust teachers to fulfil an impartial role.

Young people were very passionate about coming up with solutions in relation to alcohol misuse. This seemed to be an opportunity for them to express their personal opinions and debate the issues with other young people. It illustrated that drinking is not an isolated issue for young people and must be linked to a number of social care arenas.

About Turning Point

Turning Point is the UK's leading social care organisation providing services for people with complex needs across a range of health and disability issues. It is the largest provider of substance misuse treatment services and a major provider of mental health and learning disability services.

- The above information is the executive summary of *Alcohol consultation with young people in England, 2004*. The consultation was led by Turning Point's Hungerford Project and funded by Comic Relief. For more information please contact Turning Point. See page 41 for their address details.

© Turning Point

Drinking to excess rising among women

In 2002/03, around two-thirds of adults aged 16 and over in Great Britain had had an alcoholic drink on at least one day during the previous week (74 per cent of men and 59 per cent of women).

Nearly one in three adults (30 per cent) had exceeded the recommended daily benchmark (of 4 units for men and 3 units for women) on at least one day during the previous week. Men were more likely to exceed the benchmark than women – 38 per cent of men compared with 23 per cent of women.

The proportion exceeding the daily benchmark was highest among young people aged 16 to 24 (45 per cent) and lowest among older people aged 65 and over (10 per cent). Nearly half (49 per cent) of young men aged 16 to 24 exceeded the benchmark compared with 16 per cent of older men aged 65 and over. Likewise, 42 per cent of young women aged 16 to 24 exceeded the benchmark compared with 5 per cent of older women aged 65 and over.

Across the GB regions, the proportion of adults exceeding the daily benchmark was highest in the North East (39 per cent) followed by Scotland and Wales (35 per cent). The lowest percentages were in London and the East of England (25 per cent), the South East and the West Midlands (27 per cent).

Heavy drinking (defined as above 8 units for men, and above 6 units for women, on at least one day in the last week) follows a very similar age pattern to drinking above the daily benchmark. Among both men and women, young people aged 16 to 24 were the most likely to drink heavily (35 per cent of men and 28 per cent of women) and older people aged 65 and over the least likely to drink heavily (5 per cent of men and 1 per cent of women).

Trends over time are only available for the previous guidelines of weekly recommended benchmarks (21 units for men, 14 units for women). Since the late 1980s there has been an increase in the proportion exceeding this level, almost entirely due to an increase among women. The proportion of women exceeding the weekly benchmark increased from 10 per cent in 1988/89 to 17 per cent in 2002/03 compared with an increase from 26 per cent to 27 per cent for men over the same period.

Drinking above the weekly benchmark increased across all age groups among women, but most markedly among young women aged 16 to 24. Their rate more than doubled from 15 per cent in 1988/89 to 33 per cent in 2002/03. This compared with an increase from 31 per cent to 37 per cent over the same period for young men of the same age.

Drinking above the recommended guidelines leads to increased risk of harm, both immediately and in later life. High levels of drinking play a part in mortality due to accidents and a number of diseases, including cirrhosis of liver, heart disease, strokes and some cancers.

In 2000, there were 11,800 drink-drive accidents in Great Britain, resulting in 530 deaths. It is estimated that there were 5,543 alcohol-related deaths in total in England and Wales in 2000.

Sources:
General Household Survey, Office for National Statistics for drinking data. Recent trends in alcohol-related mortality, and the impact of ICD-10 on the monitoring of these deaths in England and Wales, *Health Statistics Quarterly* 17, Office for National Statistics for alcohol-related deaths data.

Road Casualties Great Britain 2002: Annual Report, Department for Transport for road accidents data.

Notes:
In 1992, the Government introduced the weekly guideline that men should drink under 21 units per week and women under 14 units per week. In 1995, the guidelines were changed from weekly to daily, advising that men should drink no more than 4 units per day and women no more than 3 units per day. A unit is defined as 8 grams of alcohol which is equivalent to half a pint of ordinary strength beer, a small (125ml) glass of wine (at 9 per cent strength) or one measure of spirits.

The GHS figures before 1998/99 are unweighted and from 1998/99 onwards are weighted.

■ The above information is from the Government's statistics web site: www.statistics.gov.uk

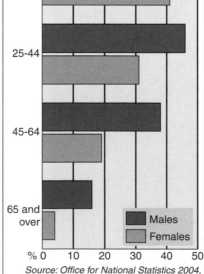

Drinking to excess

Adults exceeding recommended daily benchmarks of alcohol at least once during the last week, 2002/03, Great Britain

- Males
- Females

Source: Office for National Statistics 2004, Crown copyright

'Ladettes' clog casualty units after catfights

The number of women who are seeking treatment at hospital casualty units after being injured in drunken catfights is rising sharply, consultants warn.

Late-night brawls between women who have been binge drinking are resulting in horrific injuries such as facial wounds caused by 'glassing', broken jaws and bleeding scalps, where girls have had their hair pulled out.

Hospital staff, already under pressure from the rising numbers of emergency admissions, say that they are struggling to cope with a 'disturbing' increase in the number of intoxicated women requiring treatment. In some areas, the number of admissions has tripled in five years.

Don MacKechnie, the chairman of the British Medical Association's accident and emergency committee and a consultant at Rochdale Infirmary in Lancashire, said that casualty units were being inundated with injured young women, particularly at weekends.

'There has certainly been a big increase and some of the fights are really vicious,' he said. 'It is not just cuts and grazes, but fractured hands as a result of them punching other people, and broken cheekbones.'

By Julie Henry and Michael Day

Amjid Muhammed, a consultant at Calderdale Royal Infirmary in Halifax, West Yorkshire, said that about 45 of the 300 patients seen in accident and emergency over a typical weekend were women wounded in drunken brawls. Five years ago, the typical figure was less than 15.

> *Late-night brawls between women who have been binge drinking are resulting in horrific injuries such as facial wounds, broken jaws and bleeding scalps, where girls have had their hair pulled out*

He blamed the threefold rise on the increasing tendency of groups of young women to binge drink. 'There are women who are intoxicated who are hurting themselves by toppling over or having an accident. Then there are women who are injured in fights. It used to be men but now women are turning up in this state – and even worse than the men in some cases,' he said.

Mr Muhammed said that one worrying new trend was 'glassing' – women hitting other females with glasses or bottles. 'That was something we never used to see, but I have seen a few cases recently,' he said. 'It causes quite serious injuries – a facial glassing can be very nasty.'

Mr Muhammed said that drunken women were putting pressure on already stretched A & E departments. 'They are adding to the growing numbers of people that are coming in that need to be seen. Every extra patient adds to the queue.'

The extent of the spiralling workload facing Britain's casualty units was underlined earlier this month by figures from the Department of Health showing that the number of admissions rose by up to a third in some hospitals in the second quarter of this year, compared with the same period last year.

The rising tide of female violence has been blamed on the growing 'ladette' drinking culture,

where women ape the worst excesses of loutish male behaviour. Recent Government statistics have revealed that almost a third of 18- to 24-year-old women binge drink.

Last year, a report produced for the Prime Minister's Strategy Unit estimated that treating illness and injuries caused by alcohol cost the National Health Service £1.7 billion a year. According to doctors, an increasing amount is spent on treating women.

Lt Col Andrew Cope, a consultant at Peterborough District Hospital, said that he was dealing with a rising number of women injured in drunken fights.

'We tend to have the stereotypical image of the male alcoholic, but women are now involved too,' he said. 'We have seen women hitting each other with glasses and bottles. The trouble is mainly at weekends and bank holidays, when people have too much to drink and get out of control.'

A consultant from Sunderland Royal Hospital said that a quarter of the 300 admissions in a busy 24-hour period were alcohol-related and were as likely to involve women as men.

A spokesman for Brighton and Sussex University Hospitals NHS Trust said that women sustaining injuries while drunk was an 'ongoing problem' at weekends.

A study by the Schools Health Education Unit in Exeter published in August 2004 found that teenage girls were now drinking more alcohol than boys.

Research by Lancaster University published in September 2004 showed that children as young as 13 are displaying such 'ladette behaviour'. Teachers interviewed in the study said that girls were drinking at earlier ages and had become aggressively assertive and arrogant.

One teacher from a secondary school in the north of England said: 'Their life is about going out and drinking, and it starts very early. I was shocked when I found out that some of the 13- and 14-year-olds quite regularly go out drinking at the weekend.'

A pupil at the school described girls in her class as 'fighting a lot, punching each other and pushing,

swearing and spitting on each other. You don't go near them because they will batter you, just like a lad.'

Alcohol Concern, an organisation that campaigns to reduce alcohol abuse, accused the drinks industry of targeting women through advertising and the development of 'women-friendly, attractive drinking venues'.

A spokesman for the Portman Group, which speaks for the drinks industry, denied that it glamorised alcohol, however.

'There are now more than a million women who drink more than six units in a session,' she said.

'As part of our "Don't Do Drunk" campaign we are appealing to women's vanity. We concentrate on what drinking does to their appearance and their skin, as well as reminding them of the more serious risks of chronic disease and the dangers of being assaulted or having accidents while drunk.'

© Telegraph Group Limited, London 2004

Alcohol and crime

Information from Alcohol Concern

- Research shows that alcohol is a factor in criminal behaviour. In 2003 in the UK nearly two-thirds of sentenced male prisoners (63%) and four-fifths of female sentenced prisoners (39%) admitted to hazardous drinking prior to imprisonment.
- It is estimated that alcohol-related crime costs the UK £7.3 billion per annum in terms of policing, prevention services, processing offenders through the criminal justice system and human costs incurred by the victims of crime.
- In a 2003 MORI poll, 78% of respondents said they were concerned about binge-drinking, drunkenness and disorderly behaviour and only 25% of respondents aged 35 to 54 visited their town centres in the evening once or more than once a week.
- 69% of male binge-drinkers and 45% of female binge-drinkers reported at least one violent incident in the last year compared to 34% of regular male drinkers and 18% of regular female drinkers.
- Of the estimated 60,000 sentenced prisoners in the UK, just over 40,000 are hazardous alcohol users. Almost half of these have severe alcohol problems.
- It is possible to 'design out' alcohol-related disorder by using measures such as Pub- and Club Watch schemes banning troublemakers from nightlife areas; door staff training and registration schemes; cutting back on irresponsible drinks promotions; safety audits of licensed premises to improve the physical environment; use of toughened glass to prevent broken glasses or bottles being used as weapons; CCTV in and around late-night venues; provision of late-night transport.
- Since 2000, the Government has implemented a range of legislation and initiatives aimed at reducing alcohol-related crime and disorder.

- This is a summary of a detailed factsheet which is available from Alcohol Concern's information unit. Many other factsheets are also available. Visit their website at www.alcoholconcern.org.uk

© Alcohol Concern

Call for pubs to cover cost of policing drunks

Pubs and clubs should pay the police and local authorities up to £30,000 a year to help tackle crime and disorder caused by excessive drinking, the former Home Office minister John Denham said today.

Mr Denham, who chairs the Commons home affairs select committee, said the government should allow police and local councils to impose a charge of up to £30,000 a year on licensed premises in town centres to fund extra policing.

His comments came as charities which provide care and support to people affected by excessive drinking expressed concern that the government's long-awaited alcohol harm reduction strategy would prove ineffective.

The strategy, published today, calls for pubs and clubs to make voluntary contributions towards the cost of policing areas, such as town centres, affected by alcohol-fuelled antisocial behaviour and offending. It also ordered a review of alcohol advertising to ensure manufacturers did not glamorise drinking or encourage underage drinking.

But Mr Denham said tougher action was required to ensure that the most profitable drinking establishments carried a 'fair share of the cost' of town-centre binge drinking.

'The money raised should be used to fund additional police officers, community support officers and local authority wardens,' he said.

'In too many communities, too much of the recent increased number of police are being taken up policing city-centre drunkenness. This prevents the police giving the priority they would like to residential areas.

'A sensible scheme might cover about 6,000 of the 110,000 licensed premises, with the levy ranging between a few hundred pounds a year for the smaller premises and over £30,000 for the super-clubs. The levy would raise enough to provide

an additional 1,800 police officers at weekend, or an equivalent cost in civilian staff.'

The proposal was backed by the charity Alcohol Concern, which called for a tax on alcohol advertising to help fund health campaigns promoting sensible drinking.

Only £95m a year is spent on alcohol services, compared to £500m for drugs. Alcohol is a far greater problem in the UK

The charity's chief executive, Eric Appleby, said: 'We'd go even further [than the government] by introducing a 3%-5% levy on the alcohol industry's £200m annual advertising spend – to be fed back into health campaigns on alcohol.'

Other charities and medical experts added that the government would need to invest more money in treatment services if the alcohol strategy was to properly address Britain's binge drink culture.

Lesley King-Lewis, the chief executive of the charity Action on Addiction, said alcohol services were currently underfunded.

She said: 'Only £95m a year is spent on alcohol services, compared to £500m for drugs. Alcohol is a far greater problem in the UK with over 5,000 deaths directly attributable to alcohol and as many as 33,000 alcohol-related deaths a year, but only just over 1,000 directly related to the use of illicit drugs.'

Lord Victor Adebowale, chief executive of social care charity Turning Point, said the strategy did not address the 'chronic lack of alcohol treatment services for the 3.8 million people who are dependent drinkers'.

He said: 'The document today gives little concrete hope of speedier, more effective treatment to the people who want to deal with their alcohol dependence.

'This is small comfort for the families of the 13 people who will die today, as every day, as a direct result of alcohol misuse.'

■ The above article first appeared in the *Guardian*, 15 March 2004.

© *Press Association*

Crime and disorder

Prevalence of offending in last 12 months for those aged 18 to 24, by sex and drinking status

Percentages	Binge drinker			Other regular		
	Men	Women	All	Men	Women	All
Any offence in last 12 months	49	22	39	21	8	14
Violent crime	25	3	17	7	1	4
Taken part in a group fight in a public place	22	2	15	6	1	3
Theft	16	4	11	10	3	6
Criminal damage	7	<1	4	1	0	0
Base no.	212	143	355	176	205	381

Source: Findings 185, Home Office. Crown copyright

Drink, drugs and driving

Driving under the influence of drink and drugs remains a serious concern for Britain's motorists. It is estimated that 3,000 people are killed or seriously injured each year in drink-drive accidents. Since the 1970s, successive governments have worked to increase awareness of the dangers of drink-driving

Drunk driving

The general consensus is that these campaigns have been successful, and the UK now has a strong anti drink-driving culture:

- More than 9 in 10 motorists believe that driving when over the legal limit is a dangerous and extremely serious crime.
- Only 1% of motorists admitted to driving when over the alcohol limit in the last 12 months – yet, this still equates to approximately 200,000 drivers who have drink-driven in the last year.
- Motorists display a high awareness of the maximum legal alcohol levels for driving and most err on the side of caution. Over 80% of motorists believe the legal alcohol level for the maximum amount of wine and spirits that may be drunk before driving to be lower than it actually is.
- While the majority of motorists do not engage in drink-driving, most drivers believe there is an ongoing need to deter those who persist in driving while over the limit.
- Motorists feel that current laws provide a powerful enough deterrent. Yet, 5 in 10 motorists believe that the one factor likely to reduce drink-driving is stricter enforcement of the current drink-driving laws.
- 8 in 10 motorists support the introduction of random breath testing.
- Over 1 in 3 strongly agreed that the legal drink-drive limit should be reduced to 'no alcohol at all'; in comparison only 1 in 5 strongly supported halving the limit.

The morning-after

Despite the progress made, driving after drinking heavily the night before, or 'morning-after motoring' remains a key concern – 6% of motorists admit to getting into a car in the last 12 months where the driver had been drinking heavily the night before:

- 'Morning-after motoring' is perceived as much less dangerous than driving on the same day when over the blood alcohol limit. 7 in 10 motorists stated that driving after drinking heavily the night before is extremely or very dangerous, compared to 9 in 10 for driving over the legal limit on the same day.
- Despite the perception that 'morning-after motoring' is less dangerous than 'same day' drink-driving, only a small proportion of motorists believe that it should be officially classed as a less serious offence.
- Young drivers and company car drivers are more likely to have been in a car where they knew the driver had been drinking heavily the night before.

■ The above information is a summary of the Report on Motoring 2003 – *Drink, Drugs and Driving* produced by the RAC. For more information visit the RAC's website which can be found at www.rac.co.uk

© *2004 RAC Motoring Services*

Drinking and driving

Have you ever heard of the designated non-drinking driver campaign/promotion?

Yes	60.4%
No	39.6%

Have you ever been the designated non-drinking driver or nominated a non-drinking driver?

Yes	56.3%
No	43.7%

Do you think campaigns that encourage the idea of a designated driver can help reduce drink driving?

Yes	88.9%
No	11.1%

What do you think are the advantages of being a designated non-drinking driver?

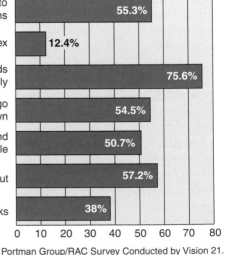

Shows you're doing your bit to reduce drink drive injuries and deaths	55.3%
You're more attractive to the oppositive sex	12.4%
You make sure your friends and family get home safely	75.6%
You and your friends can go to new places out of town	54.5%
Encourages others that drinking and driving is socially unacceptable	50.7%
It saves me money when I go out	57.2%
People tend to buy me drinks	38%

Base: 820 18- to 30-year olds, interviewed by telephone December 2003   Source: Portman Group/RAC Survey Conducted by Vision 21.

Alcohol advertising

Ofcom revises rules on alcohol advertising

Ofcom has announced new draft rules on the television advertising of alcoholic drinks. The subject has been debated for some time, often heatedly. It has been felt by many clinicians and people working in the field of alcohol policy that the drinks industry was getting away with a great deal too much, especially when aiming its advertising towards young people. A particular area of concern has been the use of sexual images and the implication of enhanced sexual performance or attractiveness.

The industry has become increasingly aware that it was open to criticism and has been active in making attempts to forestall any move towards statutory regulation of advertising. Its problems, of course, have been less immediate in the United Kingdom, where the Government listens very closely to what the industry and its front organisation, the Portman Group, have to say.

The draft rules which now appear were drawn up in response to views expressed, inevitably, by the drinks industry and also by consumer groups that existing rules, inherited from the Independent Television Commission, were insufficiently focused with regard to:

■ Discouraging advertising likely to be strongly attractive to children and young teenagers.
■ Discouraging advertising which appears to condone anti-social behaviour related to drinking, particularly with implications of excess consumption.
■ Discouraging an implied linkage between drinking alcohol and sexual success. As far as concessions go, the industry has made small steps towards stating the glaringly obvious and now agrees to do what it might well have been expected to be doing all along. Alcohol advertising on television has been subject to specific rules since the beginnings of commercial

television in the United Kingdom. In 2003, Ofcom's predecessor, the Independent Television Commission, had research carried out to assess whether the current rules remained effective and appropriate. Ofcom states that it 'has taken forward that research, whose principal elements include:
– Two reviews of academic literature which indicate that alcohol advertising has some impact on young people's attitudes to alcohol. However, this is at a relatively low level compared to other influences within the wider family and social environment.
– A qualitative study which indicates that a good deal of television advertising – of alcopops in particular – is closely aligned to youth culture and of strong interest to underage drinkers. However, the research demonstrates that advertising which does not seek to make a linkage with youth culture and which features older people is much less attractive for children and younger teenagers.'

The first point minimises clear evidence that alcohol advertising does influence young people. No one would argue that the social environment and family have a greater effect but that is not to say that there is not an obligation on advertisers to ensure that their products are not made attractive to under-age drinkers.

The second point makes two unconnected statements in a manner which implied that the second mitigates the first, which, of course, it does not. The barest familiarity with alcohol advertising makes it abundantly evident that a substantial proportion of it is strongly aimed at young people. The fact that the proportion aimed at older customers is unappealing to youth is neither here nor there.

Ofcom states that it 'has reviewed the current rules in light of the research findings. It is now seeking views on proposals to strengthen the rules. The proposals are targeted at the following specific issues:

■ Condoning anti-social or self-destructive behaviour.
■ Linking alcohol with sexual activity or attractiveness.
■ Reducing the appeal of the advertising to young audiences.
■ Condoning the irresponsible handling or serving of alcohol.'

In March 2004 the Cabinet Office identified television advertising of alcoholic drinks as one of many potential factors relevant to its wider strategy on alcohol harm reduction. Ofcom believes that 'the evidence from the research, combined with the views of stakeholders, indicates that a tightening of the existing rules on defined aspects of alcohol advertising would be proportionate and would be likely to make a contribution to that wider strategy'. Nevertheless, indications are that Ofcom will shy away from suggesting further statutory regulation of the drink industry and its advertising, leaving it to the system of self-regulation for which the industry has campaigned so vigorously. Those who have observed the influence exercised by the industry during the passage of the new Licensing Act and the formulation of the Alcohol Harm Reduction Strategy will not be surprised.

The full consultation document and related research is available on Ofcom's website at www.ofcom.org.uk

■ The above information is from an edition of *Alert*, the magazine produced by the Institute of Alcohol Studies. For further information, visit their website which can be found at www.ias.org.uk

© *Institute of Alcohol Studies*

Alcohol and the night-time economy

Information from Alcohol Concern

■ The advantages and dis-advantages of alcohol's impact on the night-time economy are hotly contested issues. This information examines the positive and detrimental effects of drinking on the evening leisure culture. It considers what can be done to manage the worst excesses of alcohol misuse.

■ The evening leisure industry is huge, as illustrated by the following:
– There are currently 110,000 on-licence premises in England and Wales, an increase of 30% over the last 25 years
– Applications for on-licences are running at 5000 per annum, an increase of over 145% over equivalent licences granted in 1980
– The pub and club industry turns over £23 billion per year – equal to 3% of the UK Gross Domestic Product.

■ The night-time economy can

benefit a local community by stimulating the refurbishment declining areas – a range of bars, restaurants and clubs attracts visitors and tourists, while at the same time improving facilities for local residents. Food and drink establishments also provide employment opportunities for the community.

■ Among the negative effects of the night-time economy is that it offers more opportunities for people to binge-drink and engage in anti-social behaviour. Consuming large quantities of alcohol in a short space of time is particularly common among 18- to 24-year-olds and drinkers put themselves at increased risk of having accidents, are more likely to take sexual risks and behave anti-socially.

The wider community suffers from aggressive, drunken behaviour, increased noise and litter and increased pressure on the emergency services.

■ This is a summary of a detailed factsheet which is available from Alcohol Concern's information unit. Many other factsheets are also available. Visit their website at www.alcoholconcern.org.uk Alternatively see page 41 for their address details.

© *Alcohol Concern*

24-hour drinking 'will fuel crime'

By Philip Johnston,
Home Affairs Editor

Allowing pubs and clubs to open all hours could lead to a rise in violent crime, disorder and nuisance, says a leaked report from the Metropolitan Police.

It fears more drink-driving because of the lack of public transport late at night, a boom in illegal cabs and taxi touts, a growth in street vendors operating in the black economy and greater disturbance to residents.

Varied closing hours will encourage people to go out later and force the police to patrol trouble spots throughout the night, it says.

Ministers argue that more flexible opening will help reduce disorder by stopping clubs and pubs emptying at the same time.

But the report by the Met's clubs and vice operational command unit, passed to the *Telegraph*, challenges the entire Government strategy for curbing binge drinking and anti-social behaviour.

While the Home Office is emphasising the need to contain excessive drinking, the Department for Culture, Media and Sport is pressing ahead with laws to introduce more flexible opening times.

From the summer of next year, these will allow pubs to open into the small hours or round the clock in some cases. Responsibility for licensing will be transferred from magistrates to councils. Guidelines on implementing the legislation are due to be published in a few weeks.

Councils will have to consider the impact on the neighbourhood of late-night opening before sanctioning it. Police will be able to close down premises that regularly attract trouble.

The Met's report is concerned with London, especially the West End, but police chiefs across the country are thought to share its misgivings about the Licensing Act 2003.

The report says: 'The Government's assertion that closing time and binge drinking are linked is valid, but closing time is not the only causal factor.'

It predicts a rise in pub crawls through the night.

'A further complication will be that, with premises remaining open longer, transient drinking will take place. This will increase the numbers of persons on the street.

> **With more drunks on the streets for longer, the police fear a rise in fights, rape, robberies, domestic violence and assaults on officers**

'Whilst it is accepted that staggered closing may induce a gradual drift away from premises, it is unlikely to reduce the numbers that use premises. The flashpoints that traditionally occur between 11pm and 5am may be reduced in intensity but occur with increased frequency.'

With more drunks on the streets for longer, the police fear a rise in fights, rape, robberies, domestic violence and assaults on officers.

The report cites the experience of several European cities, including Dublin where flexible hours were introduced four years ago.

It says: 'With the drinking culture that is firmly entrenched in the country, the relaxations in permitted hours will for the foreseeable future fuel this culture.'

David Davis, the shadow home secretary, said the Government should ensure that existing laws against under-age drinking were properly enforced before extending the opportunity for bingeing.

Drinking, crime and disorder

Findings from the Youth Lifestyles Survey

- 39% of 18- to 24-year-olds were classified as 'binge drinkers' (those who got very drunk at least once a month). Men were more likely to binge drink (48%) than women (31%).
- Binge drinkers were more likely to offend than other young adults. 39% reported committing an offence in the 12 months prior to interview, compared with 14% of regular drinkers. Young male binge drinkers were particularly likely to offend (49%).
- 60% of binge drinkers admitted involvement in criminal and/or disorderly behaviour during or after drinking, compared with 25% of regular drinkers. Again young males were most likely to report such behaviour (69%).
- The link between drinking and offending was particularly strong for violent crimes.
- Even after other factors were taken into account, frequency of drunkenness remained strongly associated with both general offending and criminal and disorderly behaviour during or after drinking.

- The above information is an excerpt from Findings 195, *Drinking, crime and disorder*, from the Home Office.

Alcohol sharpens your brain, say researchers

*By Robert Matthews,
Science Correspondent*

It is news guaranteed to raise a cheer among those who enjoy a glass or two: drinking half a bottle of wine a day can make your brain work better, especially if you are a woman.

Research published in August 2004 by academics at University College London has found that those who even drink only one glass of wine a week have significantly sharper thought processes than teetotallers.

The benefits of alcohol, which are thought to be linked to its effect on the flow of blood to the brain, can be detected when a person drinks up to 30 units of alcohol – about four to five bottles of wine – per week.

The researchers were unable to test the effect of higher levels of alcohol consumption, although drunkenness probably negates any positive effects on the brain.

The findings have surprised health officials, who issued yet another warning in August 2004 about the dangers of overdrinking.

According to figures released by the Office for National Statistics, one in six women now drinks more than the Government's recommended limit of 14 units of alcohol a week – an increase of 70 per cent since the late 1980s. The recommended maximum weekly intake for men is 21 units.

The latest findings on the benefits of alcohol are drawn from a study of the long-term health of 10,000 British civil servants. Known as the Whitehall Study, it was originally set up in 1967 to identify links between health and factors ranging from smoking and obesity to age and social status.

In the latest research, a team led by Sir Michael Marmot, a professor of epidemiology and public health at University College London, gave psychometric tests to more than 6,000 civil servants.

The questions ranged from verbal and mathematical reasoning problems to tests of short-term memory. The civil servants' performance was then matched against their drinking habits.

The study took into account all alcohol consumption and was not specific to wine. However, the results showed that those having even a single glass of wine a week scored significantly higher in the tests than more abstemious drinkers. Teetotallers were twice as likely as occasional drinkers to achieve the lowest scores.

The benefits were most marked among women drinkers and, to the researchers' surprise, showed no sign of flattening out with increasing consumption.

Those who downed the equivalent of half a bottle of wine or two pints of beer a day scored best of all. The effects were apparent even after the results had been adjusted to take into account factors such as physical and mental health.

'Our results appear to suggest some specificity in the association between alcohol consumption and cognitive ability,' said the team. 'Frequent drinking may be more beneficial than drinking only on special occasions.'

The team, whose findings are being reported in the *American Journal of Epidemiology*, suggests that the results may reflect the fact that alcohol can reduce the risk of cardiovascular disease and increase blood flow to the brain – factors linked to improved mental function.

The researchers also speculate that women might benefit more because of the different way in which they metabolise alcohol. However, they acknowledge that the benefits of alcohol can be outweighed by the increased risks of getting diseases such as cancer and cirrhosis, and that the findings should not be used as an excuse for heavier drinking.

Dr Guy Ratcliffe, the medical director of the Medical Council on Alcohol, said that the study would add to earlier evidence that moderate drinking could be beneficial – offering advantages such as a reduced risk of heart disease and strokes.

'This is a well-researched study, and it's important that information such as this is available so that people can make informed decisions about alcohol consumption,' he said.

Kate Winstanley, the policy director of the Portman Group, set up by the industry to promote responsible drinking, welcomed the findings.

'There is a lot of concern about trends in women's drinking, especially young women, but the concern is chiefly about women who drink to get drunk. This study does seem to support the view that moderate drinking is better than none at all,' she said.

The University College team is now hoping to continue the study to investigate whether alcohol can help slow the decline of mental function as people grow older. A recent American study suggested that drinkers suffered significantly less cognitive decline with age than teetotallers, with women again showing the greatest benefit.

© *Telegraph Group Limited, London 2004*

Responsible drinking

Information from the Portman Group

Moderate drinking in appropriate circumstances presents little or no harm to the drinker and can even provide health benefits.

The following advice is based on the Government's responsible drinking message as set out in *Sensible Drinking – The Report of an Inter-Departmental Working Group*.

Men

Most men can drink up to three to four units of alcohol a day without significant risks to their health. For men aged 40 and over there is evidence that drinking one to two units a day, but no more, can reduce the risk of coronary heart disease.

Women

Most women can drink up to two to three units of alcohol a day without significant risk to their health. Women who are trying to conceive or who are pregnant should avoid getting drunk and are advised to consume no more than one to two units of alcohol once or twice a week. After the menopause there is evidence that drinking one to two units a day, but no more, can protect against the risk of coronary heart disease.

Most people enjoy drinking and find it a sociable and relaxing thing to do. Normally it leads to no harm. But there are times when drinking too much – or even drinking at all – can cause problems. For example:

Don't . . .

- drink and drive;
- operate machinery, use electrical equipment or work at heights after drinking;
- drink before playing sport or swimming;
- drink while on certain medications – check labels and ask a doctor if unsure;
- binge drink – it can lead to health and other problems.

Do . . .

- abstain for 48 hours, if you do have an episode of heavy

Promoting Responsible Drinking

drinking, to let your body recover;
- remember drinks poured at home are often bigger than pub measures;
- work out how much you drink and try to stick to the guidelines – which are daily benchmarks not weekly targets;
- get help from a doctor or a specialist agency if worried about your drinking;

- remember that drinking responsibly can be enjoyable and is compatible with a healthy lifestyle.

Visit our web site for more information about responsible drinking advice, read about our campaigns, try our online unit calculator or to look up the answers to the most frequently asked questions about responsible drinking. Women who are pregnant or planning to conceive should read our page on pregnancy and drinking. To order any of our materials on responsible drinking, use our online catalogue or call us on 020 7907 3700.

- The above information is from the Portman Group's web site: www.portman-group.org.uk

© Portman Group

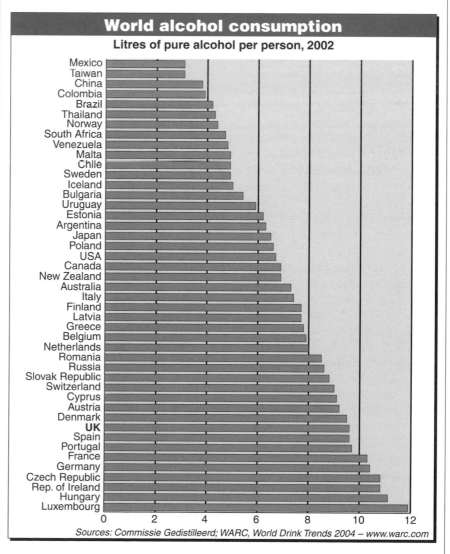

World alcohol consumption
Litres of pure alcohol per person, 2002

Mexico, Taiwan, China, Colombia, Brazil, Thailand, Norway, South Africa, Venezuela, Malta, Chile, Sweden, Iceland, Bulgaria, Uruguay, Estonia, Argentina, Japan, Poland, USA, Canada, New Zealand, Australia, Italy, Finland, Latvia, Greece, Belgium, Netherlands, Romania, Russia, Slovak Republic, Switzerland, Cyprus, Austria, Denmark, **UK**, Spain, Portugal, France, Germany, Czech Republic, Rep. of Ireland, Hungary, Luxembourg

0   2   4   6   8   10   12

Sources: Commissie Gedistilleerd; WARC, World Drink Trends 2004 – www.warc.com

Alcohol

Information from the Royal College of Psychiatrists

Introduction

Alcohol is our favourite drug. Most of us use it for enjoyment, but for some of us, drinking can become a serious problem.

Most people don't realise that alcohol causes much more harm than illegal drugs like heroin and cannabis. It is a tranquilliser, it is addictive and it helps to cause many hospital admissions for physical illnesses and accidents.

Problems with alcohol

Many of these problems are caused by having too much to drink at the wrong place or time. They include: fights, arguments, money troubles, family upsets, spur-of-the-moment casual sex. Alcohol can make you do things you would not normally do. Drinking alcohol can help cause accidents at home, on the roads, in the water and on playing fields.

Problems with alcohol – physical health

Being very drunk can lead to severe hangovers, stomach pains (this is called gastritis), vomiting blood, unconsciousness and even death. Drinking too much over a long period of time can cause liver disease and increases the risk of some kinds of cancer. But there is good news for men over 40 and women of menopausal age – for them very moderate drinking may reduce the risk of heart disease.

Problems with alcohol – mental health

Although we tend to think of alcohol as something we use to make us feel good, heavy drinking can make you badly depressed. Many of the people who commit suicide have drinking problems. Alcohol can stop your memory from working properly and in extreme cases cause brain damage.

In some people alcohol can cause them to hear imaginary voices. This is usually a very unpleasant experience and can be hard to get rid of.

Warning signs

Alcohol is addictive. It is a bad sign if you find you are able to hold a lot of drink without getting drunk. You know you are hooked if you do not feel right without a drink or need a drink to start the day.

Dealing with alcohol problems

If you are worried about your drinking or a friend's drinking, then you should take steps to make changes as early as possible. It is much easier to cut back before drinking problems damage your health than it is once they are out of hand.

First steps

It may be enough to keep a diary of your drinking and then to cut down if you find you have been drinking too much. It helps if you can talk your plans over with a friend or relative. Do not be ashamed to own up to the problem. Most real friends will be pleased to help and you may find they have been worried about you for some time.

Getting help

If you find it hard to change your drinking habits then try talking to your GP or go for advice to a council on alcohol. If you feel you cannot stop because you get too shaky or restless and jumpy, then your doctor can often help with some medication for a short time. If you still find it very difficult to change then you may need specialist help.

Changing habits

We all find it hard to change a habit, particularly one that plays such a large part in our lives. There are three steps to dealing with the problem:

- Realising and accepting that there is a problem.
- Getting help to break the habit.
- Keeping going once you have begun to make changes.

It is at this stage that you may find that you have been using alcohol as a way of handling stress and worries. A psychiatrist or a psychologist may be able to help you find ways of overcoming these worries that do not involve relying on drink.

Groups where you meet other people with similar problems can often be very helpful. Groups may be on self-help like Alcoholics Anonymous or arranged by an alcohol treatment unit.

Most people dealing with their drink problems do not need to go into hospital. Some people will need to get away from the places where they drink and the people they drink with. For them, a short time in an alcohol treatment unit may be necessary. Drugs are not used very often except at first for 'drying out' (also known as 'detoxification'). It is important to avoid relying on tranquillisers as an alternative.

Most people with drinking problems are just like the rest of us, but there are some who are going to need extra help, such as the homeless. They may need a place to stay while they kick the habit and make a new start in their lives.

Although beating a drink problem may be hard at first, most people manage it in the end and are able to lead a normal life.

- The above information is from the Royal College of Psychiatrists' website which can be found at www.rcpsych.ac.uk

© Royal College of Psychiatrists

Sensible drinking

Information from Alcohol Focus Scotland

Why should I control my drinking?

Alcohol is a drug and just like any other drug, its use can sometimes lead to problems.

But I'm not an 'alcoholic'

Many people have an image of what they think someone looks like who has a drink problem, but in actual fact anyone can experience an alcohol-related problem.

- It doesn't matter what age or sex you are, or what occupation or lifestyle you have.
- You don't need to have a dependence or 'need' of alcohol to have a problem.
- People who drink regularly and heavily or aim to get drunk may also have a problem through: accidents; violence; workplace problems; relationship problems; problems with the law and other health-related problems.

How much can I safely drink?

Women:
2-3 units per day
– but not every day and no more than 14 units in total for the week.

Men:
3-4 units per day
– but not every day and no more than 21 units in total for the week.

Can I just keep my 'safe weekly total' for a Friday night?

This is sometimes called binge drinking, where large amounts of alcohol are drunk on one occasion, and:

- Increases your risk of having an accident.
- Can lead to serious health problems.
- Can result in alcohol poisoning which means that parts of the brain which control the automatic functions like heartbeat and lungs are affected.*
- A second effect of alcohol poisoning can be through choking on vomit by being too 'out of it' for your reflexes to work.*
- Doing or saying things which you regret once you've sobered up, like arguing with friends or having sex which you later regret.

* Anyone who is difficult to rouse should be given immediate medical attention.

Some tips

Before and during drinking

- Avoid mixing alcohol with other drugs or medication.
- Have something to eat before you start drinking – food in the stomach allows alcohol to be absorbed more slowly.
- Avoid drinking to get drunk – stay in control of yourself.
- Be careful about drinking in 'rounds'. You tend to end up drinking at the speed of the fastest drinker in the company.
- Learn to refuse offers of drinks which you don't want.
- Drink slowly and space alcoholic drinks out with soft drinks.
- Avoid drinking competitions or gimmicky events to get you to drink more.
- If you feel hungover after drinking don't be tempted to take alcohol to help you feel better. Take lots of non-alcoholic fluids, rest and stay off alcohol for 48 hours and you'll feel much better.
- Avoid using alcohol to help you cope with situations like shyness or insomnia, as alcohol causes disturbed sleep patterns.

Talk to someone you trust about developing confidence to ease the shyness.

- Using alcohol to help you cope with problems will only blot them out – it won't actually solve them.

- Rather than drinking as your only method of winding down try to ensure you've a range of options for relaxing.
- Your body needs 48 hours to recover after a heavy drinking session.
- Aim for at least two alcohol-free days per week.

But they say alcohol's good for you!

Research suggests that small amounts of alcohol (1-2 units per day) can reduce the risk of heart disease in men over 40 or women who are past the menopause. But remember, the same benefits can be achieved through a healthy diet and exercise.

Younger people, generally, are less likely to suffer from heart attacks, therefore there are no medical benefits for this age group.

When shouldn't people drink?

Alcohol has an effect on your reaction time, judgement and co-ordination.

This means that it's dangerous, to yourself and others, to drink while:
- Driving

- Doing sports
- Using machinery
- Working

As well as:
- During pregnancy & when breastfeeding (1)
- With certain medications (2)

(1) If you choose to have a drink during pregnancy, this should be no more than 1-2 units, once or twice a week.

(2) Check with your doctor or pharmacist.

Note – alcohol dulls the action of the brain and, although this may feel stimulating at first, it actually has a depressant effect.

How do I know if I've got a problem?

The following is not a complete list but may indicate a problem:
- Are you aware that you're now drinking more? If so, think about why this is.
- Do you need time off work due to a hangover or regularly have a hangover?
- Using alcohol to block out feelings or thoughts?
- Having arguments with friends or family about your drinking?
- Drinking to 'cure' a hangover?

In Scotland, 33% of males and 15% of females exceed the recommended weekly limits of alcohol consumption.

If you're concerned about your own or someone else's drinking, contact Alcohol Focus Scotland for further information or information on the alcohol advice agency nearest to you.

- The above information is from Alcohol Focus Scotland's website which can be found at www.alcohol-focus-scotland.org.uk

© *Alcohol Focus Scotland*

Living with a drinker

Information from TheSite.org

Alcoholism is a destructive force, affecting more than 2 million UK households. Why? Because it doesn't just affect the drinker, but everyone around them.

Here's what you can do when someone close to you is drinking to excess:
- You can't make someone stop drinking. They have to recognise the problem first, and only then can they decide to face up to it.
- If you're worried then share your concern with them, and even encourage them to open up about any underlying problems. Make them aware of the problems their drinking is causing to others, and listen to why they feel the need to reach for the bottle. Just choose your moment wisely, preferably when they're sober.

- Don't attempt to control their habit by hiding bottles or pouring alcohol away, as you could end up with an angry confrontation on your hands.
- Alcohol can make people behave unpredictably. If there's a risk of violence, take steps to protect yourself.
- Whatever has caused this person to turn to drink, you are not to blame. Nor should you feel

---

Alcoholism is a destructive force, affecting more than 2 million UK households

---

obliged to cover up for their habits or make excuses about it to others.

More info

Sometimes, the only way to help is by helping yourself, so tell someone you trust about what's going on, or call Drinkline on 0800 9178282 and consider your options with a trained counsellor.

National Association for Children of Alcoholics (NACOA)

Provide information, advice and support to children of alcoholics, or anyone else concerned for a friend or relative's drinking. Helpline: 0800 358 3456

- The above information is from TheSite's website which can be found at www.thesite.org

© *TheSite.org*

Doctors see an alcoholic a day

But there's no more cash to help

By Jamie Doward and Jo Revill

The Government has been accused of ignoring an impending health crisis after it emerged last night that a long-awaited report into combating alcohol misuse rules out more cash for treating people with drink problems.

Ministers were accused of capitulating to big business after Whitehall sources revealed that the Alcohol Harm Reduction Strategy, to be published on 12 March, also rules out slapping tobacco-style compulsory health warnings on drink.

Alcohol awareness groups reacted with dismay to the news and said that, according to the Government's own figures, alcohol misuse cost £20 billion a year in lost productivity and NHS bills – while drugs misuse cost £18.8 billion. Yet only £95 million a year was spent treating alcoholics compared with £500 million a year treating people with drugs problems.

Health workers say this lack of cash has led to an acute shortage of detox beds and rehabilitation clinics, which means obtaining treatment is often a lottery, based on where an alcoholic lives. While the average GP sees 360 patients a year who are misusing alcohol, in fewer than 5 per cent of cases is there any kind of intervention – partly because of the shortage of centres where patients can be sent for appropriate help.

To news there would be no extra cash for treatment, Peter Martin, chief executive officer of Addaction, which helps people with drug and alcohol problems, said: 'If this is the case, then we are very worried at the shortsightedness of some in government. We are concerned about what the consequences of doing nothing now will mean for future generations.'

A survey of alcohol users, to be published by Addaction next month, has found a 20-year gap between people developing a drink problem and seeking treatment. The gap has fuelled an alarming rise in alcohol-related deaths.

Government statistics show that in 1980 alcohol accounted for 2 per cent of deaths among 15- to 44-year-olds. Now it accounts for 7 per cent of deaths among men and 6 per cent among women. Among young men especially, there has been a sharp rise in premature alcohol-related deaths – from 2,101 in 1993 to 3,800 in 2001.

The Government had mooted forcing the drinks industry to finance alcohol awareness campaigns and print health warnings. But those who have seen the report say the Government has opted to let the industry – which contributes £7 billion a year to the Treasury – draw up its own voluntary code of good practice.

The climbdown follows a battle between the Department of Trade and Industry and the Home Secretary, David Blunkett, who favoured regulation.

Addaction's Martin said: 'We think some in government take this issue very seriously and want to see the industry do far more. But government has probably got to encourage the drinks industry to play their part and see what they are

prepared to do voluntarily. But the industry has got to share the risk that society bears on alcohol misuse.'

The drinks firm Diageo had recently spent £100 million advertising Smirnoff vodka worldwide. One-eighth of this would purchase beds in detox for two weeks for 15,000 people.

One way of targeting alcohol misuse would be to increase taxation to the point where it impacts on sales. The idea is outlined in a report, *Calling Time: The nation's drinking as a major health issue*, to be published this week by the Academy of Medical Sciences.

Professor Michael Marmot, chair of the Academy's working group and a renowned expert on alcohol policy, said the report demonstrates the link between the growing alcohol consumption in the UK and anti-social behaviour. But it concludes that increasing levels of heavy drinking 'are not irreversible', and points to initiatives that produced a marked shift in behaviour, such as the drink-driving campaigns of the Eighties and Nineties, which made it socially unacceptable to drink before getting behind the wheel of a car.

Last year the Chancellor froze, for a sixth Budget, the duty on spirits, but put 1p on a pint of beer and 4p on a bottle of wine. This means that the average family in Britain now spends around £112 a year on alcohol duty.

Although many public health officials would like to see taxes rise further, the move would be unpopular with the public, who feel that alcoholic drinks are expensive compared with the rest of Europe.

The drinks industry has argued that higher British prices simply increase smuggling and also help wine importers.

■ This article first appeared in *The Observer*, 29 February 2004.

The NACOA Helpline

Making a difference in the lives of children of alcoholics

The National Association for Children of Alcoholics (NACOA) was set up in 1990 to address the problems experienced by children growing up in families were one or both parents suffer from alcoholism, or a similar addictive problem.

Our current research indicates that there are 920,000 children and young people under the age of eighteen, living in the UK today with one, or perhaps both parents who have a problem with alcohol. Of these, 644,000 will try to hide the problem from the outside world.

It is clear from research studies that alcoholism as an outcome is but one risk factor for the offspring of an alcoholic. For children of alcoholics the home environment is very often characterised by inconsistent parenting, with unpredictable rules and limited, chaotic or tense family environments; parental violence and spouse abuse; unpredictability; broken promises; loneliness and isolation as family members attempt to hide the family's problems. Research also shows that the degree to which children are able to shelter themselves from the negative impact of alcoholism plays an integral part in their growing up to be well-adjusted adults.

Although some alcohol services offer family-based therapies for families, there are few services, which offer help for the vastly greater number of children who suffer from the problematic drinking of parents who neither acknowledge nor seek help for their problems. These children find themselves with no one obvious they can turn to for help. NACOA addresses this need by providing information, advice and support through our free telephone helpline, website www.nacoa.org.uk and supporting services.

Loneliness, fear and confusion are the three problems reported most often by children of alcoholics calling the NACOA helpline. Fourteen-year-old Tim, told one of NACOA's volunteer counsellors:

By Hilary Henriques, Chief Executive of NACOA

'Sometimes I don't think anyone sees me. I feel so alone and so different from the other kids in my class. I used to try to talk to my Mum but that would upset her. I was frightened when I saw my Dad lying passed out on the floor but Mum said "it's all right". So we ignored him and pretended that nothing's wrong, although we know there is. We walk around him, we have tea in the kitchen and we can't watch television because we mustn't wake him up. We all pretend it's normal but I know it's not.

'We are all happier when he is sleeping because things are calm for a while, although we are dreading him waking up. What will he be like when he wakes up? Will he be angry or happy? Will he go to the pub or to the shed to start drinking again leaving us to worry until he passes out again? We replay the same game over and over in our heads. What will he be like when he wakes up, dad or some raging drunk who hates us, who blames me for his problems – if only I could do better at school, then maybe he would not have to drink.'

Tim is one of 7,284 callers to the helpline in 2002-2003. Tim's family life is torn apart by violence, by failing relationships, by constant arguments, by financial hardship and by constant neglect of the little things that are so crucial.

The NACOA helpline provides the anonymity and safety needed by children who may be afraid to ask for help, feel they are betraying their parents or think they will not be believed. There are no magical solutions but every caller is counselled as an individual with individual problems and needs; not simply an extension of a parent's drinking problem. We use a five-step approach, researching services and resources from our library and databases of information, collated over the past fourteen years.

For Tim

- we listened and helped him to explore the problems he faces and his feelings in a non-judgemental way
- we provided information on alcoholism, stressing he was not to blame, that he could not stop his father drinking but he could do something for himself
- we helped him to work out what he could and could not do, both for his father and himself. We

helped him to find new ways of coping and ways to have a life for himself irrespective of whether his father continued to drink, or not

- we helped him to work out who he could talk to – people he could trust with his private thoughts and feelings – and also who he could not trust
- we referred Tim to a local drop-in centre for young people in his area and introduced him to youth groups and other activities so he could start to enjoy himself outside the family home

Tim's father still drinks but Tim knows now that he is not alone. He is still frightened by his father's drunken rages but he knows that he can go to his friend's house, without having to explain anything and go home when he feels safe. Tim is still confused by his Mum who continues to try to ignore his Dad's drinking but he now trusts his own feelings and feels happier that the problem is not his fault or in his imagination. Tim continues to call the helpline when he wants or needs to – he knows we will be here for him and will help him to face problems. He is not alone.

- NACOA welcomes calls from children of alcoholics of all ages and anyone concerned for their wellbeing.

For further information please contact: Helpline 0800 358 3456 Mon to Fri 10.00 am to 7.00 pm. E-mail: helpline@nacoa.org.uk Web site: www.nacoa.org.uk Admin 0117 924 8005 Mon to Fri 10.00 am to 4.00 pm. E-mail: Admin@nacoa.org.uk

- For information about the NACOA training programme for helpline volunteers, or other volunteering opportunities please call 0117 924 8005 or email volunteering@nacoa.org.uk.

- The above article first appeared in an edition of *Alcohol Alert*, a magazine produced by the Institute of Alcohol Studies. For further information see their address details on page 41.

© Institute of Alcohol Studies

Drinking problems 'are out of control'

Cases of liver disease caused by excessive drinking soared by 75 per cent in six years and cost the NHS more than £65 million a year, the Liberal Democrats said 1 January 2004. 'Alcohol-related illness is spiralling out of control,' said Paul Burstow, the party's health spokesman.

The Lib Dems attacked the Government for delaying its alcohol strategy for six years. 'Ministers have done nothing to tackle the growing cost of excessive drinking both in terms of health and to the taxpayer,' said Mr Burstow.

'The culture of binge drinking among young people, particularly women, is damaging their health. Much more needs to be done to alert people to the health risks.' He added: 'The Government's alcohol strategy was announced in 1998 but still has not been published.'

According to the Government's own statistics in 2002-03, 151,086 'bed days' were taken up in NHS hospitals by people with alcohol-related problems.

The Lib Dems said that not only were more people being treated for liver diseases but that their problems were more severe, needing longer stays in hospitals.

In 1996-97 the average length of stay in hospital for a patient with alcoholic liver disease was 12.7 days. By 2002-03 this was 14.1 days.

Six years ago hospital consultants gave 10,903 treatments for alcohol-related liver diseases compared with 19,130 in 2002-03. A government report in September estimated that 17 million working days were lost to hangovers and the cost of treating alcohol-related injury and illness was £1.7 billion.

Recommendations from the Alcohol Harm Reduction Strategy group were expected at the end of this year, for implementation next year.

- Almost half of all revellers planning to take drugs on New Year's Eve will mix alcohol with a cocktail of illegal substances, a poll revealed 1 January 2004.

The findings were announced by Frank, the Government's campaign to fight drug misuse. Partygoers are being urged to avoid mixing alcohol and drugs.

© Telegraph Group Limited, London 2004

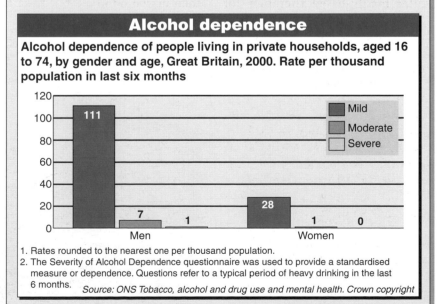

Alcohol dependence

Alcohol dependence of people living in private households, aged 16 to 74, by gender and age, Great Britain, 2000. Rate per thousand population in last six months

Men: Mild 111, Moderate 7, Severe 1
Women: Mild 28, Moderate 1, Severe 0

1. Rates rounded to the nearest one per thousand population.
2. The Severity of Alcohol Dependence questionnaire was used to provide a standardised measure or dependence. Questions refer to a typical period of heavy drinking in the last 6 months. *Source: ONS Tobacco, alcohol and drug use and mental health. Crown copyright*

Tips for cutting down

Are you worried that you may be drinking too much? Do you want to cut down? These useful tips will help you.

First start by working out what you drink in a week by reviewing the last week. If it is difficult to remember keep a daily note for the next week. Note all the drinks, how many units in each, the times of day and where you were. If this is a typical week, your notes should give you a good idea about whether you are drinking too much and, importantly, the situations in which you drink and whether it's going to be hard to cut down

If you think your drinking is a problem, try following these steps:

Step one

Decide what your aim is. Do you want to give up alcohol altogether? Or do you want to cut down to within daily benchmarks? Or maybe you want to avoid binge-drinking and all the problems that go with it. The decision is yours but be clear about what you want to achieve.

Step two

Pick a day in the next week to start cutting down. Go for a day when you are likely to be relaxed and not under pressure. Plan ahead for a day when it is easier to avoid alcohol.

Step three

Work out how you can avoid situations when you know you end up drinking more. If you often drink at home, stock up on alternatives to alcohol, like alcohol-free beers, or lagers or wine or soft drinks. You might like to tell other people that you are cutting back, this should avoid them putting pressure on you to drink and they might even join in.

Step four

Do not give up! Changing habits like drinking takes time and hard work and sometimes it is difficult to drink less. Keep focusing on the positive things you have achieved. If you do relapse, set a new date to start reducing again.

Step five

If you continue to find it difficult to cut down you could see a trained alcohol counsellor to help you develop strategies or contact Drinkline for advice

---

Are you worried that you may be drinking too much? Do you want to cut down? These useful tips will help you

---

Tips for cutting down

Keep a drink diary. Keeping a drink diary on a regular basis will help you to work out how much you are drinking and give you some idea of what situations make you drink more.

Stick to the limit you have set yourself. Work out a reasonable drinking limit for any day when you drink and stick to it. Set a limit for particular occasions like parties or Friday nights at the pub or wine bar.

Watch what you drink at home. Most people pour larger drinks at home than the ones in pubs or bars. Buy smaller glasses and take care not to go over your target. Avoid heading straight for a drink when you get home, take a thirst-quenching soft

drink or cup of tea and give yourself some time to relax after coming through the door.

It is OK to say no. Do not let anyone pressurise you into having another drink. If you think saying no could be difficult, have some excuses lined up such as 'No thanks, I have had enough' or 'I have got a lot on tomorrow'.

Pace your drinks. Try drinking more slowly and putting the glass down in-between sips. Choose smaller drinks like halves instead of pints. Avoid strong brands. Try spacing out alcoholic drinks by alternating them with soft drinks or low strength alcoholic drinks. Avoid rounds as they often mean you drink more than you want. Skip some rounds by drinking more slowly. Or when it is your round, choose an alcohol-free drink for yourself.

Occupy yourself while you are drinking. Find something else to do like playing darts or pool. These will distract you from drinking and help you to drink slowly.

Find alternatives. Get out of the habit of drinking because you are tense, upset or have nothing else to do. Look for other ways to relax which will make you feel better and don't involve alcohol.

Have alcohol-free days. If you are trying to cut down, having days off proves to yourself that you are in control of your drinking.

Reward yourself. Chart your progress. Cutting down requires willpower and self-control so you should be pleased with yourself for succeeding. Buy yourself something special with the money you save from not drinking. Be honest with yourself. Make sure you only reward yourself when you meet the targets you set yourself.

■ The above information is from Alcohol Concern's information unit. For further information visit their website: www.alcoholconcern.org.uk

© Alcohol Concern 2004

Alcohol harm reduction strategy: main points

The government has published its alcohol harm reduction strategy for England; these are the main findings and proposals

Findings

- Nearly 40m people in Britain consume alcohol – more than 90% of the adult population.
- The alcohol market is worth £30bn a year; it generates one million jobs and excise duties are worth £7bn a year.
- More than half of those adults drink within sensible guidelines but one in three men and one in five women exceed the recommended levels of alcohol consumption.
- The deaths of an estimated 15,000 to 22,000 people every year are linked to alcohol.
- Drinkers under 16 are consuming twice as much alcohol as 10 years ago and are more likely to get drunk than their European counterparts.
- Binge drinking cost the UK £20bn a year; it accounts for 40% of all men's drinking sessions.
- Up to 150,000 hospital admissions a year are alcohol related and alcohol abuse is estimated to cost the NHS £1.7bn a year.
- There are 1.2m incidents of alcohol-related violence and 97,000 cases of drink driving.
- Up to 17m working days are lost annually by alcohol-related absence costing up to £6.4bn a year.

Proposals

- Police will be encouraged to make greater use of existing powers, such as exclusion and antisocial behaviour orders, to ban problem drinkers from pubs and city centres, and fixed penalty fines for those causing a nuisance on the streets.
- Pubs and clubs will be asked to pay towards the costs of policing crime and disorder caused by excessive alcohol consumption, and the creation of city centre marshals to patrol areas such as taxi ranks and late-night bus stops.
- The drinks industry will be asked to make financial contributions to alcohol educational programmes and research.
- Drinks manufacturers will be encouraged to introduce better labelling of alcohol levels in drinks.
- The communications watchdog Ofcom will investigate alcohol advertising.
- Better training to help NHS staff identify alcohol problems at an earlier stage and refer people for treatment before they get worse.
- The Department of Health will set up pilot projects to better identify people with alcohol problems.
- The Commission for Health Audit and Inspection should monitor alcohol treatment services.
- The Department of Health should set up a website to provide employers with advice on dealing with staff who appear to have alcohol problems.
- An audit of what treatments are available for alcoholics, which are most effective and whether supply matches demand.
- There will be a review of drug and alcohol education in schools to improve its effectiveness.

- The above article first appeared in the *Guardian*, 15 March 2004.

© Press Association

> *Binge drinking cost the UK £20bn a year; it accounts for 40% of all men's drinking sessions*

— IT'S NOT ALL BEER AND SKITTLES OUT HERE...

Teenagers to help tackle under-age drinking

By John Carvel, Social Affairs Editor

Undercover squads of teenagers are to be sent into pubs, clubs and supermarkets to identify premises selling alcohol to under-age drinkers, under plans due to be announced by ministers today (15 March 2004).

After a four-year review of policy, the government will publish a national alcohol strategy to combat an epidemic of binge drinking that is costing the nation £20bn a year.

Hazel Blears, Home Office minister, will call on the drinks industry to clean up its act by halting 'irresponsible promotions' such as happy hours when prices are cut to encourage maximum consumption.

The manufacturers will be told they are themselves drinking in the last chance saloon and will face a statutory clampdown if they do not volunteer reform.

David Blunkett, home secretary, had been urging Tony Blair to include in the document a list of sanctions that would be introduced if the firms failed to co-operate, including powers to fix prices in city centres and charging landlords for policing.

But the prime minister, with backing from the Treasury and the culture department, feared this could be interpreted as anti-business. A leak of Mr Blunkett's proposals in the *Sunday Times* may have served the purpose of motivating the manufacturers more efficiently, and he was said to be happy with the outcome last night.

The leak said he wanted powers to fix alcohol prices in city centres to curb excessive drinking, even though it might break competition law.

He wanted a compulsory levy on pubs and clubs worth an average £10,000 a year to pay for up to 30,000 extra police officers. And he hoped to instruct councils to refuse new licences to premises unless the applicants could prove they would not increase antisocial behaviour.

Instead Ms Blears will announce a tightening of existing controls. She will urge the police to step up action against teenage drinkers and their suppliers and will ask local authorities and the drinks industry to co-operate. The Home Office will consider how to legitimise entrapment of suppliers by sending youngsters under 18 to buy alcohol.

> **Drinkers under 16 are consuming twice as much alcohol as 10 years ago and are more likely to get drunk earlier than their European peers**

She wants city centre marshals to police problem areas and late-night bus stops where violence flares.

The plan is based on a scheme in Manchester where 100 civilian public protection officers have been brought in to supplement 20 police patrolling the city centre, creating a safer environment.

The government will encourage manufacturers to introduce better labelling of alcohol levels in drinks, but that would be voluntary at this stage. Further measures might emerge in a public health white paper later this year on which John Reid, health secretary, is consulting.

The strategy document will note that nearly 40 million people in Britain consume alcohol – more than 90% of the adult population. The market exceeds £30bn and generates one million jobs. Excise duties on alcohol are worth £7bn a year. Over half the adult population drinks within sensible guidelines. But almost one in three adult men and one in five women exceed the guidelines.

Drinkers under 16 are consuming twice as much alcohol as 10 years ago and are more likely to get drunk earlier than their European peers.

In the UK, binge drinking accounts for 40% of all men's drinking sessions. Up to 150,000 hospital admissions a year are alcohol-related and alcohol abuse is estimated to cost the NHS £1.7bn a year.

There are 1.2m incidents of alcohol-related violence and 97,000 cases of drink driving, costing up to £7.3bn a year. Up to 17m working days are lost annually due to alcohol-related absence, costing up to £6.4bn a year, the government will say.

The charity Turning Point called on ministers to do more to tackle a chronic lack of treatment for alcohol abuse. Lord Victor Adebowale, its chief executive, said: 'We are fighting a losing battle. The advertising budget alone for beers, wines and spirits is three times the amount spent on treating alcohol dependency – enough to fund 170,000 detox places.'

Double drink prices, urge doctors

By Celia Hall, Medical Editor

Doctors called 5 March 2004 for the price of alcohol to be almost doubled in an attempt to reduce the harm caused by excessive drinking.

The Academy of Medical Sciences, an independent body of senior doctors and researchers, has concluded that attitudes to drinking need to change.

The best way to cut the amount people drink is to limit the affordability and availability of alcohol, they say.

The doctors' leader, Prof Sir Michael Marmot, said: 'Alcohol is a good friend and a bad enemy. We are not against alcohol. It gives pleasure and also confers health benefits.'

However, the academy argues that drinking levels should return to those of the early 1970s when the population drank on average seven litres of alcohol per head a year. This compares with the 11.1 litres now consumed. The figures represent a rise of 50 per cent in 30 years.

They say there is a direct link between the relative cheapness of alcohol and the increasing amounts consumed.

The doctors have called for the price of beer, wine and spirits to be increased to 1970 levels. In relative terms alcohol was nearly twice as expensive 30 years ago, they say.

Sir Michael, professor of epidemiology and public health at the University College London, said such measures would have a greater impact on the pockets of young people who drank too much than on people who drank sensibly. 'We believe that if you can reduce the average you will also be able to do something about the heavy drinkers,' he said.

'A strategic programme is needed to curb the nation's escalating level of drinking in the interests of individual and public health. The country has reached a point where it is necessary and urgent to call time on runaway alcohol consumption.'

The academy's report, *Calling Time*, also proposes limits on the amount of alcohol people can bring in from Europe and lower drink-driving limits – down from 80mg per 100ml of blood to 50mg and to zero for drivers younger than 21.

The report says the current travellers' allowance gives a heavy drinker a 272-day supply.

They say this should be reduced to the permitted level of nicotine imported for personal use which gives a 20-a-day smoker a 40-day supply.

'Educational approaches have been disappointing but this may be swamped by contrary advertising,' the report says. 'Price modulation usually through tax increase is highly effective, particularly in under-age drinkers.'

'A 10 per cent rise in the price of all alcoholic beverages has been estimated to reduce mortality from alcohol-related conditions by seven to 37 per cent.'

Prof Ian Gilmore, registrar of the Royal College of Physicians and a member of the working party, accepted that their recommendations would not please politicians. 'The report makes it very clear that targeting problem drinkers is not sufficient,' Prof Gilmore said.

'It collects the compelling evidence that one of the most effective ways of reducing harm to individuals is to reduce the escalating national consumption of alcohol.

'This challenge makes alcohol an issue for society as a whole, and we encourage a wide debate on the policy options of proven benefit, such as increasing price and limiting access, unpalatable to politicians though they may be'. The doctors said that drinking at levels of one or two drinks a day provided proven health benefits but that higher amounts began to do harm.

Deaths from chronic liver disease had risen from 124 in men and 86 in women, aged 45 to 54, in 1970 to 805 and 405 respectively in 2000. Alcohol is responsible for 70 per cent of cirrhosis deaths.

Prof Gilmore said: 'I now see liver cirrhosis in people in their 20s and 30s, pretty women, who think they will get a warning sign. But the first thing you know is that you go yellow and your belly swells up. People are not just drinking more, they are drinking younger.'

The report says that over 30 years chronic liver disease has escalated by more than 450 per cent.

A spokesman for the Department of Health said the Cabinet was producing its own report on reducing harm caused by alcohol in the next few weeks.

Got a drink problem?

Nobody likes to admit that drink has got the better of them. Check out the facts right here, and learn to recognise the warning signs

Know your limits

The amount of alcohol a person consumes is measured in units. Here are some rough examples of what makes up a typical unit:

- Half a pint of beer or cider
- A small glass of wine
- A single measure of spirits (e.g. whisky, vodka, rum or gin)

As a rule, health experts recommend that adult men drink no more than 21 units per week, and women 14 units. In real terms, this means blokes shouldn't exceed 2 pints of lager/beer, or 3 glasses of wine a day, while women should avoid going beyond a pint or a couple of glasses. Why? Because the male body is made up of 66% fluid, compared to 55% for women. This means alcohol is more diluted in a man's body than a woman's. As a result, women tend to get drunk faster than men on the same amount of alcohol.

Waking up to the warning signs

If you're unsure whether you exceed your weekly unit allowance, try setting up a drinking diary for a while. Be sure to include every drink, the amount, the occasion, and where possible the alcohol by volume. Also make a note of whether you had a hangover and how that affected your day. That way you can build up a picture of your drinking habit, and work out whether things might be slipping out of control. Other warning signs include:

- Drinking larger amounts to get the same effect.
- Doing things when you're drunk that you go on to seriously regret.
- Missing an appointment because of a hangover.
- Binge drinking (going without for some time, and then drinking excessively in one period).

If you're unsure whether you exceed your weekly unit allowance, try setting up a drinking diary for a while

---

If you go beyond the recommended number of weekly units, or you can regularly see yourself in any of these signs, it's time to think about cutting down. If the following points sound familiar, however, then you may well have developed a drink-dependency pattern that requires professional help:

- Boozing in secret, or playing down how much you drink.
- Thinking about alcohol a lot, and when you'll next get a chance to drink.
- Getting into trouble as a result of alcohol (i.e. accidents or violence).
- Finding yourself in debt because of the amount you spend on alcohol.
- Becoming anxious when you can't get access to drink.
- Thinking you need a drink to help deal with certain situations.
- Getting into arguments or having accidents because of booze.
- Evading questions about your alcohol intake, or feeling uncomfortable about responding at all.
- Reacting angrily when people suggest you have a drink problem.

Advice and support

Al-Anon Family Groups UK and Eire
Understanding and support for families and friends of problem drinkers, whether the person is still drinking or not. Helpline: 020 7403 0888

Drinkline
Confidential telephone help, info and advice on all aspects of alcohol use and abuse. Calls are free. Telephone: 0800 9178282

- The above information is from TheSite's website which can be found at www.thesite.org

© TheSite.org

Wide-eyed and legless?

Call for better alcohol education – as youngsters stagger into their parents' footsteps

Underage teenage drinkers are staggering into their parents' footsteps, according to a new study. Lager and spirits are their favourite tipples – and most of their drinking takes place either at home or in pubs.

These are among the key findings to emerge from a report looking at the drinking habits of 15- to 17-year-olds, published by Alcohol Concern and the National Addiction Centre. The study is called *Teenage Drinkers*.

The research – which tracked the drinking patterns of 540 young people from five secondary schools over 18 months – also revealed that one in ten of the youngsters felt drinking disrupted their education at crucial GCSE stage, as well as their health and family life. Among other findings were that:

- 59% were drinking once a week at the start – growing to 80% by the end of the research
- 84% of the end sample admitted to being drunk recently
- 36% claimed not to have been asked for proof of age before the study started

The three most common negative consequences associated with alcohol were feeling sick, drinking more than planned and saying something they regretted

Commenting on the research, Alcohol Concern's Chief Executive Eric Appleby said: 'It is clear from the study that many youngsters are simply drifting into patterns of drinking set for them by their parents and friends – rather than making informed decisions about what, where and how much they drink. We would like to see this countered by more, and more imaginative, education about alcohol. This doesn't mean counter-productive preaching at young people. There have, for example, been a number of excellent "peer" projects – where teenagers find their own ways of telling their contemporaries about the dangers of excessive drinking.'

Dr Annabel Boys of the National Addiction Centre added: 'It seems that many teenagers have already adopted a fairly "adult-style" of alcohol use well before they reach

---

It is clear from the study that many young-sters are simply drifting into patterns of drinking set for them by their parents and friends

---

the legal age of 18 – and in many cases they don't feel a need to hide this behaviour from their parents. We need to face facts – the majority of teenagers drink before they are 18 and we aren't going to stop them by telling them it's bad for them. Instead we should be focusing on helping to ensure that they are equipped to make "adult-style" informed decisions about their drinking habits and can avoid getting into difficulties as a result of their drinking.'

■ The above information is from Alcohol Concern's website which can be found at www.alcoholconcern.org.uk

© Alcohol Concern 2004

More young people get help for drink problems on-line

The internet is proving to be the most popular source of help for young people seeking assistance for their drink problems. In April, Alcoholics Anonymous volunteers started handling on-line requests for help from problem drinkers for the first time ever via the Fellowship's website (www.alcoholics-anonymous.org.uk) The on-line service was set up to complement the traditional AA telephone helpline (0845 769 7555), which operates nationally with local responders.

The first three months following launch of the new Internet service shows that the on-line audience is significantly younger than the traditional AA membership (according to a recent survey, 5% of AA members are under 25). Of the 10,500 people visiting the 'AA newcomers' section of the website every month, 3,500 (33%) people click through for the 'message for young people' information. Early results of the on-line experience would indicate that the Internet is providing a convenient access point to AA for young people. According to a recent survey, 5% of AA members are currently under 25.

Since the re-launch of the AA website in April more than 500 organisations have linked their websites to the Alcoholics Anonymous site, taking advantage of the full resources the Fellowship provides for problem drinkers.

Alcoholics Anonymous was established in the 1930s in America and arrived in Britain 55 years ago. There are now more than 3,500 AA meetings every week in England, Scotland and Wales.

■ The above information is from Alcoholics Anonymous' website which can be found at www.alcoholics-anonymous.org.uk

© Reprinted with the permission of the General Service Board of Alcoholics Anonymous (Great Britain) Limited

---

- Alcoholic drinks consist mainly of flavoured water and ethyl alcohol (ethanol). They are made by the fermentation of fruits, vegetables or grains. (p. 3)

- What is a unit?:
  - One pint of normal strength lager (3-3.5%) is equivalent to 2 units
  - One 275ml bottle of alcopop (5.5%) is 1.5 units
  - a 175ml glass of 12% wine is 2 units
  - a single measure of spirits (40%) is 1 unit. (p. 3)

- New MORI research reveals that 78% are concerned (43% 'very concerned') about binge drinking, drunkenness and disorderly behaviour among British people. Yet only 7% of men and 22% of women know that the current recommended allowances are 3-4 units and 2-3 units respectively. (p. 5)

- 'While alcohol remains a Cinderella issue – a poor relation to drugs in terms of investment in treatment and education – it is hardly surprising that there are low levels of understanding about how much alcohol is healthy.' (p. 5)

- Problems of excessive drinking affect everyone. It can cause abusive behaviour and lead to violence particularly where large groups meet. You can end up hurting people you care about or causing a serious accident. (p. 6)

- The World Health Organisation's Global Burden of Disease Study finds that alcohol is the third most important risk factor, after smoking and raised blood pressure, for European ill-health and premature death. (p. 8)

- Alcohol is responsible for up to 150,000 hospital admissions each year in England and Wales. (p. 9)

- Binge drinking is where people consume more than twice the recommended daily units of alcohol, in one session, at least once a week – which is the equivalent of at least a bottle of wine. (p. 10)

- A study for an alcohol misuse charity, by the market analysts Datamonitor, has found that the average 18- to 24-year-old British woman consumes almost three and a half times as much alcohol as Italian women of the same age. (p. 10)

- Generally it is illegal for a landlord or bar manager knowingly to sell alcohol to anyone under the age of 18. It is illegal for someone over 18 to buy or attempt to buy alcohol for someone under 18. It is also an offence for someone under 18 to buy or attempt to buy alcohol for themselves. (p. 11)

- A hangover is basically alcohol dehydrating the body. The only sure way to avoid a hangover is not to drink too much. (p. 13)

- Department of Health figures show that 3,322 children aged between 11 and 15 were admitted for alcohol-related problems. Some 2,760 were taken in for mental and behavioural disorders, with 562 suffering from alcohol's toxic effects. (p. 15)

- Last year, a report produced for the Prime Minister's Strategy Unit estimated that treating illness and injuries caused by alcohol cost the National Health Service £1.7 billion a year. According to doctors, an increasing amount is spent on treating women. (p. 20)

- Research shows that alcohol is a factor in criminal behaviour. In 2003 in the UK nearly two-thirds of sentenced male prisoners (63%) and four-fifths of female sentenced prisoners (39%) admitted to hazardous drinking prior to imprisonment. (p. 20)

- Only £95m a year is spent on alcohol services, compared to £500m for drugs. Alcohol is a far greater problem in the UK. (p. 21)

- Motorists display a high awareness of the maximum legal alcohol levels for driving and most err on the side of caution. (p. 22)

- Research published by academics at University College London has found that those who even drink only one glass of wine a week have significantly sharper thought processes than teetotallers. (p. 26)

- Alcohol is addictive. It is a bad sign if you find you are able to hold a lot of drink without getting drunk. You know you are hooked if you do not feel right without a drink or need a drink to start the day. (p. 28)

- Many people have an image of what they think someone looks like who has a drink problem, but in actual fact anyone can experience an alcohol-related problem. (p. 29)

- Government statistics show that in 1980 alcohol accounted for 2 per cent of deaths among 15- to 44-year-olds. Now it accounts for 7 per cent of deaths among men and 6 per cent among women. (p. 31)

- While the average GP sees 360 patients a year who are misusing alcohol, in fewer than 5 per cent of cases is there any kind of intervention – partly because of the shortage of centres where patients can be sent for appropriate help. (p. 31)

- The NACOA helpline provides the anonymity and safety needed by children who may be afraid to ask for help, feel they are betraying their parents or think they will not be believed. (p. 32)

- 'The advertising budget alone for beers, wines and spirits is three times the amount spent on treating alcohol dependency – enough to fund 170,000 detox places.' (p. 36)

- If you're unsure whether you exceed your weekly unit allowance, try setting up a drinking diary for a while. (p. 38)

ADDITIONAL RESOURCES

You might like to contact the following organisations for further information. Due to the increasing cost of postage, many organisations cannot respond to enquiries unless they receive a stamped, addressed envelope.

Alcohol Concern
Waterbridge House
32-36 Loman Street
London, SE1 0EE
Tel: 020 7928 7377
Fax: 020 7928 4644
E-mail:
contact@alcoholconcern.org.uk
Website:
www.alcoholconcern.org.uk
Works with the government, statutory and other voluntary bodies. Alcohol Concern aims to develop more and better treatment services nationally, to increase public and professional awareness of alcohol misuse and to bring about a reduction in alcohol-related problems.

Alcohol Focus Scotland
2nd Floor, 166 Buchanan Street
Glasgow, G1 2LW
Tel: 0141 572 6700
Fax: 0141 333 1606
E-mail: enquiries@alcohol-focus-scotland.org.uk
Website: www.alcohol-focus-scotland.org.uk
Alcohol Focus Scotland is Scotland's national alcohol charity and its leading voice on alcohol issues.

Alcoholics Anonymous (AA)
General Service Office
PO Box 1, Stonebow House
Stonebow
York, YO1 7NJ
Tel: 01904 644026
Fax: 01904 629091
Website: www.alcoholics-anonymous.org.uk
Alcoholics Anonymous is a fellowship of men and women who share their experience, strength and hope with each other that they may solve their common problem and help others to recover from alcoholism.

BNTL Freeway
Westbrook Court
2 Sharrow Vale Road
Sheffield, S11 8YZ
Tel: 0114 267 9976
Fax: 0114 267 9976
E-mail: info@bntl.org
Website: www.bntl.org
Works to educate and encourage children and young people in the principles of a lifestyle free from alcohol and other drugs.

DrugScope
Waterbridge House
32-36 Loman Street
London, SE1 0EE
Tel: 020 7928 1211
Fax: 020 7928 1771
E-mail: services@drugscope.org.uk
Website: www.drugscope.org.uk
DrugScope is the UK's leading independent centre of expertise on drugs.

Institute of Alcohol Studies (IAS)
Alliance House
12 Caxton Street
London, SW1H 0QS
Tel: 020 7222 4001
Fax: 020 7222 2510
info@ias.org.uk
Website: www.ias.org.uk
Aims are to increase the knowledge of alcohol and of the social health consequences of its use and abuse. Produces a wide range of factsheets, posters, papers and books on alcohol-related issues.

Lifeline
39-41 Thomas Street
Manchester, M4 1NA
Tel: 0161 839 2075
Fax: 0161 834 5903
E-mail: mail@lifeline.org.uk
Website: www.lifeline.org.uk
Lifeline is an organisation that helps people who use drugs and the families of people who use drugs.

The Portman Group
7-10 Chandos Street
Cavendish Square
London, W1G 9DQ
Tel: 020 7907 3700
Fax: 020 7907 3710
portmangroup@compuserve.com
Website: www.portman-group.org.uk
Established by the eight leading UK drinks companies to: promote sensible drinking; reduce alcohol-related harm; and develop a better understanding of alcohol misuse.

Royal College of Psychiatrists
17 Belgrave Square
London, SW1X 8PG
Tel: 020 7235 2351
Fax: 020 7235 1935
E-mail: rcpsych@rcpsych.ac.uk
Website: www.rcpsych.ac.uk
Produces an excellent series of free leaflets on various aspects of mental health. Supplied free of charge but a stamped, addressed envelope is required.

The National Youth Agency (NYA)
19-23 Humberstone Road
Leicester, LE5 3GJ
Tel: 0116 242 7350
Fax: 0116 242 7471
E-mail: nya@nya.org.uk
Website: www.nya.org.uk
www.youthinformation.com
The National Youth Agency aims to advance youth work to promote young people's personal and social development, and their voice, influence and place in society.

Turning Point
New Loom House
101 Backchurch Lane
London, E1 1LU
Tel: 020 7702 2300
Fax: 020 7702 1465
E-mail: tpmail@turning-point.co.uk
Website: www.turning-point.co.uk
Turning Point is a social care organisation working with individuals and their communities across England and Wales.

INDEX

absenteeism, alcohol-related 35
advertising
    alcohol 2
        and anti-social behaviour 23
        and binge drinking 10-11
        budget 36
        costs of 31
        Ofcom regulations 2, 23-4, 35
        tax on 21
        and young people 23
        young people's attitude to 17
alcohol
    alcopops 3, 11, 15, 23
    and anti-social behaviour 23, 24, 31
    applications for licences 24
    attitudes to
        drink-driving 22
        excessive drinking 5, 20
    beer and lager 3, 4, 5, 8
    and brain function 26
    calories in 3
    cider 3
    composition of 3
    confronting alcohol abuse 28-39
        advice and support 38
        alcohol-free days 34
        alternatives to alcohol 34
        changing habits 28
        children of alcoholics 30, 32-3
        city-centre marshals 2, 36
        dealing with alcohol problems 28
        doctors and the treatment of alcoholics 31
        drugs for detoxification 28
        expenditure on treating alcohol dependency 36
        fixing alcohol prices 36
        getting help 28
        knowing if you have a problem 30
        living with a drinker 30
        and the NHS 35
        Pub and Club watch schemes 20
        pubs and clubs to pay cost of policing drunks 21, 35
        tackling under-age drinking 36
        tips for cutting down 34
        waking up to warning signs 38
    costs of alcohol abuse 15, 31
    deaths related to 8-9, 11, 18, 31, 35, 37
    drinks industry
        and the alcohol harm reduction strategy 35
        labelling alcohol levels 36
        Portman Group 20, 26, 27
        and under-age drinking 36
    and drugs 33
    effects of 6-7, 13
    European Comparative Alcohol Study 8
    government policies on
        Alcohol Harm Reduction Strategy 1, 5, 10, 15, 24,

        31, 33, 35, 36
        excise duty 31, 36
        Licensing Act (2003) 25
    health benefits of 9, 28, 30
    health risks of 4, 7, 8-9, 18, 26, 28
    keeping a drink diary 4, 28, 34, 38
    methyl alcohol 3
    and the night-time economy 2, 24
    prices 37
    pub and club opening hours 25
    responsible drinking 27
    sensible drinking tips 29-30
    spirits 3, 4, 5, 8
    statistics on alcohol consumption 35
    UK legislation on the sale of 11
    units of 4, 13, 38
        and heavy drinking 18
        safe limits 2, 3, 4, 10, 27, 29, 38
    Whitehall Study on 26
    wine 3, 4, 5, 8
    see also binge drinking
Alcohol Concern 5, 14, 20, 21, 24
    on teenage drinkers 39
    tips for cutting down 34
Alcohol Focus Scotland 7, 13, 29
Alcohol Harm Reduction Strategy 1, 5, 10, 15, 24, 31, 33, 35, 36
alcoholic poisoning 29
Alcoholics Anonymous 28
    and young people 39
alcopops 3, 11, 15, 23

binge drinking
    and advertising 10-11
    and alcoholic poisoning 29
    costs of 1-2, 35
    and criminal/disorderly behaviour 25
    defining 10, 38
    getting help 7
    and 'Happy Hours' 10, 11, 12, 36
    health risks of 4, 7
    and men 1, 2, 36
    public awareness of safe drinking levels 5
    public concern over 5, 20
    statistics on 35
    tips for cutting down 34
    and women 1, 10, 12, 18, 19-20
        'ladettes' 19-20
    and young people 1, 6, 10, 12
boys and young men
    and alcohol 16
        binge drinking 15

cancer, and alcohol consumption 7, 8, 18, 28
cars
    drink-driving 22, 30, 31, 35, 36, 37

morning-after motoring 22
children, of alcoholics 30
clubs
    and binge drinking 1, 2
    to pay cost of policing drunks 21, 35, 36
crime, alcohol-related 1, 5, 20, 25

deaths, alcohol-related 8-9, 11, 18, 31, 35, 37
depression, and alcohol consumption 28
diaries, keeping a drink diary 4, 28, 34, 38
doctors
    and alcohol
      call for increase in drink prices 37
      treatment of alcoholics 31
    and help for problem drinkers 28, 31
domestic violence, alcohol-related 1, 5
drink-driving 22, 30, 31, 35, 36
    call for lower limits 37
drugs, and alcohol 33

girls and young women
    and alcohol 16
      binge drinking 1, 15, 19-20
      'ladettes' 19-20
GPs (general practitioners), help for problem drinkers
    28, 31

health benefits, of alcohol 9, 28, 30
health risks
    of excess alcohol consumption 4, 7, 8-9, 18, 26, 28
      mental health 28
      and young people 17
heart disease, and alcohol consumption 7, 8, 9, 18, 26,
    27, 28, 30

Institute of Alcohol Studies 8-9
Internet, and young people with drink problems 39

life expectancy, and alcohol consumption 9
liver disease, and alcohol consumption 7, 8, 11, 18, 28,
    33, 37

men
    and alcohol
      binge drinking 1, 2, 36
      deaths from liver disease 11
      drinking above recommended guidelines 18, 35
      and hospital admissions 9
      safe limits 2, 3, 4, 27, 29, 38
mental health, and alcohol consumption 28
methyl alcohol 3
Metropolitan Police, and pub and club opening hours 25
morning-after motoring 22

NACOA (National Association for Children of
    Alcoholics) 30, 32-3
NHS (National Health Service)
    costs of treating alcoholics 31
    hospital admissions, alcohol-related 1, 9, 11, 15, 19,
      35, 36
    identification of alcohol problems 35

parents
    and alcohol
      influence on young people 17
      and young binge drinkers 12, 14
police
    and binge drinking 2, 21
    and the Government's alcohol harm reduction
      strategy 35
Portman Group 20, 26
    on responsible drinking 27
pregnant women, and alcohol consumption 4, 27
pubs
    and binge drinking 1, 2, 11
    to pay cost of policing drunks 21, 35, 36

road accidents, and alcohol consumption 7, 8, 18
rural areas, young people and drinking in 12, 14

schools
    alcohol education in 11, 16, 35
    girls and 'ladette behaviour' 20
suicide, and alcohol consumption 28

taxation
    on alcohol 31, 36, 37
      advertising 21
television advertising, alcohol 23

violence
    alcohol-related 1, 5, 25, 35, 36
      and children of alcoholics 32, 33
      and 'ladettes' 19-20

women
    and alcohol
      binge drinking 1, 10, 12, 18, 19-20
      and brain function 26
      consumption 10
      deaths from liver disease 11
      drinking above recommended guidelines 18, 35
      effects of 13
      health benefits of 9, 28, 30
      and hospital admissions 9, 19
      pregnant women 4, 27
      safe limits 2, 3, 4, 27, 29, 38
      young women 1, 15, 16, 19-20
working days, lost through alcohol-related absences 35

young people
    and alcohol 12-17
      advertising 23
      attitudes to 16, 17
      binge drinking 1, 6, 10, 12
      drinking above recommended guidelines 18
      drinking habits 12, 39
      education about 11, 16
      effects of 6-7, 13, 24
      experience of 16
      hospital admissions for alcohol abuse 15
      influence of others 16-17
      and the law 6, 11
      in rural areas 12, 14
      safety information 13
      under-age drinking 6, 15, 25, 35, 36, 39

ACKNOWLEDGEMENTS

The publisher is grateful for permission to reproduce the following material.

While every care has been taken to trace and acknowledge copyright, the publisher tenders its apology for any accidental infringement or where copyright has proved untraceable. The publisher would be pleased to come to a suitable arrangement in any such case with the rightful owner.

Chapter One: Alcohol

The massive cost of Britain's binge drinking, © Guardian Newspapers Limited 2004, *A summary of changes over time*, © Crown copyright is reproduced with the permission of Her Majesty's Stationery Office, *Alcohol*, © Drugscope, *What's what? and how much is too much?*, © Lifeline, *Binge drinking Britons*, © Alcohol Concern 2004, *How much is too much?*, © MORI, *Drinking*, © Crown copyright is reproduced with the permission of Her Majesty's Stationery Office, *Alcohol and the body*, © Alcohol Focus Scotland, *Alcohol and health*, © Institute of Alcohol Studies, *Deaths linked to alcohol consumption*, © Crown copyright is reproduced with the permission of Her Majesty's Stationery Office, *Binge drinking – are attitudes changing?*, © BNTL Freeway, *Alcohol and the law*, © The National Youth Agency, *Generation alcopop*, © The National Youth Agency, *Alcohol and young people*, © Alcohol Focus Scotland, *Drinking among pupils*, © Crown copyright is reproduced with the permission of Her Majesty's Stationery Office, *A rural battle with the bottle*, © Telegraph Group Limited, London 2004, *Nine children a day go to hospital for alcohol abuse*, © Telegraph Group Limited, London 2004, *Hospital admissions*, © Crown copyright is reproduced with the permission of Her Majesty's Stationery Office, *Young people and alcohol*, © Turning Point, *Drinking to excess rising among women*, © Crown copyright is reproduced with the permission of Her Majesty's Stationery Office, *Drinking to excess*, © Crown copyright is reproduced with the permission of Her Majesty's Stationery Office, *'Ladettes' clog casualty units after catfights*, © Telegraph Group Limited, London 2004, *Alcohol and crime*, © Alcohol Concern 2004, *Call for pubs to cover cost of policing drunks*, © Press Association, *Crime and disorder*, © Crown copyright is reproduced with the permission of Her Majesty's Stationery Office, *Drink, drugs and driving*, © 2004 RAC Motoring Services, *Drinking and driving*, © Portman Group/RAC Survey, *Alcohol advertising*, © Institute of Alcohol Studies, *Alcohol and the night-time economy*, © Alcohol Concern, *24-hour drinking 'will fuel crime'*, © Telegraph Group Limited, London 2004, *Drinking, crime and disorder*, © Crown copyright is reproduced with the permission of Her Majesty's Stationery Office, *Alcohol sharpens your brain, say researchers*, © Telegraph Group Limited, London 2004, *Responsible drinking*, © Portman Group, *World alcohol consumption*, © World Advertising Research Center (WARC).

Chapter Two: Confronting Alcohol Abuse

Alcohol, © Royal College of Psychiatrists, *Sensible drinking*, © Alcohol Focus Scotland, *Living with a drinker*, © TheSite.org, *Doctors see an alcoholic a day*, © Guardian Newspapers Limited 2004, *The NACOA Helpline*, © Institute of Alcohol Studies, *Drinking problems 'are out of control'*, © Telegraph Group Limited, London 2004, *Alcohol dependence*, © Crown copyright is reproduced with the permission of Her Majesty's Stationery Office, *Tips for cutting down*, © Alcohol Concern 2004, *Alcohol harm reduction strategy: main points*, © Press Association, *Teenagers to help tackle under-age drinking*, © Guardian Newspapers Limited 2004, *Double drink prices, urge doctors*, © Telegraph Group Limited, London 2004, *Got a drink problem?*, © TheSite.org, *Wide-eyed and legless?*, © Alcohol Concern 2004, *More young people get help for drink problems on-line*, © Reprinted with the permission of the General Service Board of Alcoholics Anonymous (Great Britain) Limited.

Photographs and illustrations:

Pages 1, 16, 35: Simon Kneebone; pages 6, 19, 38: Don Hatcher; pages 10, 29: Bev Aisbett; pages 14, 24: Angelo Madrid; pages 32, 37: Pumpkin House.

Craig Donnellan
Cambridge
January, 2005